75 A 13

GEAC

AUTHOR

HOWARTH, E.

CLASS

T64

TITLE

What a performance

What A Performance!

What A Performance!

The brass band plays . . .

ELGAR HOWARTH
AND PATRICK HOWARTH

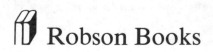 Robson Books

03242222

First published in Great Britain in 1988 by Robson Books Ltd,
Bolsover House, 5–6 Clipstone Street, London W1P 7EB.

British Library Cataloguing in Publication Data

Howarth, Patrick
    What a performance! the brass band plays.
    1. Great Britain. Music. Brass bands, to 1986
    I. Title II. Howarth, Elgar
    785'.06'71

ISBN 0–86051–474–9

Printed in Great Britain by Billing & Sons Ltd., Worcester

What A Performance!

CITY OF MANCHESTER PARKS ETC. DEPARTMENT

BAND PERFORMANCES

BOGGART HOLE CLOUGH   Sunday, May 27th, 1951

BARTON HALL WORKS BAND

(By courtesy of Messrs. L. Gardner & Sons Ltd.)

(Conductor : OLIVER HOWARTH, ESQ., A. MUS. V.C.M.)

(Vocalist : VICTOR GALVIN, Tenor)

AFTERNOON at 3 p.m.

1.	Overture ...	" The Bronze Horse "	...	*Auber*
2.	Intermezzo ...	" Tip Toe "	...	*Hetherington*
3.	Cornet Solo...	" Trumpet Concerto "	...	*Hayden*
		(Soloist : EDWIN DAWES)		
4.	Melodies from	" Pirates of Penzance "	...	*Sullivan*
5.	Xylophone Solo	" Czardas "	...	*Monti*
		(Soloist : JACK WANT)		
6.	Waltz ...	" Dance of the Young Men "	...	*Gungle*

— *I N T E R V A L* —

7.	Serenade ...	" The Panda's Picnic "	...	*Ambrose*
8.	Song ...	" The Trumpeter "	...	
		(Vocalist : VICTOR GALVIN)		
9.	Selection ...	" La Traviata "	...	*Verdi*
10.	Trombone Solo	"Angels Serenade "	...	*Goddard*
		(Soloist : MASTER STANFORD HOWARTH)		
11.	Medley	" Cavalcade of Marching Songs "		*Wright*
12.	Chorus ...	" Gloria from 12th Mass ...		*Mozart*

GOD SAVE THE KING

WHAT A PERFORMANCE!

THE BRASS BAND PLAYS...

ELGAR HOWARTH
and
PATRICK HOWARTH

CONTENTS

ACKNOWLEDGEMENTS

The authors would like to thank:

STAN HOWARTH AND Arthur Taylor for their stories, advice and ideas. All the staff and students at the National Youth Brass Band summer course in Harrogate, 1987, especially Maud Wright, Roy Newsome and David James. Our four principal interviewees, Bram Gay, Ken Hirst, Derek Bourgeois and Major Peter Parkes, for their time and hospitality. Peter and Eric Wilson and all at *The British Bandsman* for answering our queries. Moira Coleman, who typed much of the manuscript. Carolyn Fearnside for spotting mistakes, correcting our grammar and generally chivvying us along. Steven the chauffeur, Nina, Theresa, Maria, Bob, Marcus, David, Harry, Terence, and especially Mary Howarth for their constant encouragement. Many thanks also to all at Robson Books for their enthusiasm and patience.

1

Overture

Introduction

BOGGART HOLE CLOUGH still exists, I suppose, though whether there are still band concerts on Sundays through the summer I doubt. As I remember, it was a pleasant park in suburban Manchester, a good date for the Barton Hall Works Band, whose principal cornet player I was in 1951, when I was fifteen. We played twice – afternoon and evening, two hours per concert; not a famous band but a respectable 'second-section' outfit (a competition grading) based in Patricroft, just north of Salford.

Strangely enough, we didn't enter competitions (or contests, as they are known – even though, as this book will illustrate, they are generally the main focus of attention), since my father, Oliver, the conductor of the Barton Hall Works Band, did not enjoy them. Possibly he couldn't cope with the nervous strain, having been brought up in the Salvation Army, a non-competitive environment. He carried the Barton Hall members with him in this by force of personality, but in any case they were a gentle crowd, unusually teetotal in general and slightly in awe of him, since he had the ability to arrange from orchestral scores – not a very common talent at that level of banding – and he was, too, possessed of a fierce temperament in rehearsal when necessary.

The Manchester parks featured bands on all their bandstands from June until August. Not being a Championship band like, say, Fairey Aviation, Besses o' th' Barn or Wingates Temperance, who were all fairly local, we were required to give an audition, which we passed with flying colours since our repertoire was considered 'different' – my father's influence. We had, too, a personable and persuasive secretary/manager in Norman R. Petrie (I never discovered what the ever-present 'R' stood for), who saw to it that we got the better parks like Boggart, Heaton Park or Wythenshawe, whose audiences were accustomed to the likes of Foden's. Petrie was a non-player and didn't read a note of music, but was mad on the band; his type make the best managers. And we had Victor Galvin, 'late of the D'Oyly Carte Opera Company', who not only sang ballads in an agreeable light tenor voice but acted as compère, introducing the items.

It was a Northern scene: Lowry country. Within ten or twelve miles of Eccles, where we lived (Eccles of Eccles cake fame, where Bradburn's shop expertly made the genuine original like no imitation Eccles cake in the world), there must have been twenty bands at least in 1951, and bands were then thought to be on the wane. Irlam Public, Cadishead Public, Weaste Silver, Beswick Prize (who played at half-time for the Manchester United matches, to my great envy), Cheetham Hill Public, Walkden ... all of them local and, like us, in the second or third section, including our arch-rivals, Eccles Borough, a famous band fallen on lean times, once Open Champions at Belle Vue in 1930, beating Wingates and Carlisle St Stephen – big names of the day.

Salvation Army bands were common, too, existing side by side in the same small communities as their secular brothers. We, the latter, met only in contests (though Barton opted out of these, as I say) or, more excitingly for me, at the annual Whit walks in Eccles, Salford or even Manchester. Almost every church would hire a brass band to lead its Sunday school: tiny tots cool in chiffon and lace, older ones warmer in velvet and silk, the bands sweating profusely in high-necked heavy woollen military-style uniforms, labouring valiantly through the familiar marches – 'Slaidburn', 'Amparita Roca' and 'The Conqueror'.

These jobs gave opportunities to observe not only the playing but the *deportment* of our rivals – 'brown shoes', 'odd uniforms', 'untidy marching' – the bands, if unknown, being instantly and inescapably indentifiable by the name printed large round the edge of the bass drum. We observed, but we didn't mix much. Bands are tribal, keeping their secrets to themselves. Fraternizing, it was feared, led to the 'poaching' of players, the blackest crime possible.

Being a factory band, we rehearsed in the factory canteen

on Friday evenings and late on Sunday mornings. Funds were raised by a weekly raffle, which the workforce supported. The management – L. Gardiner and Sons, diesel oil engines – were not over-interested. They had bought a set of instruments years before at the band's inception, but they certainly didn't show the enthusiasm of a Foden or a Fairey, whose band members were all employed by their firms especially to play in the band, though occupying normal jobs as well. My father, in fact, was employed in the toolshed at Gardiner's, where he amused his colleagues by inventing curious musical instruments,from leftover lengths of steel pipe, on which he played tunes. My brother Stanford, a gifted trombonist, was found a job in the office, but not with the licence to practise in work-time; Gardiner's Barton Hall was less ambitious than Foster's Black Dyke Mills!

Similar enthusiasm and situations existed throughout the North, and in Scotland, Wales and the West of England too, in the industrial areas, where by 1951 bands had flourished for about a hundred years. It was an absorbing way of life, more than a hobby in our house at least, and with never a thought given to the possibilities of a musical life away from bands and into the profession – as an orchestral player, for instance. It was a world complete, and to a large extent remains so. Twenty-one years later I became the 'professional' conductor to the Grimethorpe Colliery Band, where only one player has ever shown more than a passing interest in earning his living as a musician out of the band environment; and this in spite of the example displayed by the relative few who have joined some of the most prestigious of Britain's orchestras over the years.

I was one of those rare defectors, in fact, and left the band scene with the sangfroid of the seventeen-year-old, expecting never to return until a telephone call from Ken Hirst, one of the 'soloists' of this book, stopped me in my tracks and sent me back to bands via Yorkshire, to my continuing bewilderment. The involvement I have had with the Grimethorpe band has been one of the most musically rewarding of my career, and overall certainly the happiest, for here are players of high expertise, vitally committed to their chosen form of music, deadly serious in rehearsal and performance, but with whom I have shared more laughter and friendship than any conductor normally has the right to expect.

Those twenty-odd intervening years saw changes in the band world. Old bands have died but new bands have taken their place. The big names, seemingly unstoppable, continue to dominate: Black Dyke, Brighouse and Rastrick, Fairey, GUS (formerly Munn and Felton's), Yorkshire Imperial Metals, Besses, Wingates, Cory, Grimethorpe; but even in this league, though Bickershaw Colliery is long defunct (tragic!), Rushden Temperance relegated to the lower sections and Carlton Main Frickley Colliery no longer a major force, other bands have risen, notably Desford Colliery Dowty, Leyland Motors and Stanshawe.

To the general reader these names may be unknown but, beware, banding is addictive and to the band fan – and there are thousands in Britain and tens of thousands now throughout the world – they are magical names, cause of argument, conjecture, reminiscence, pride and lifelong enthusiasm.

Enthusiasm, indeed, is the common factor. My son Patrick interviewed some of the young players in the National Youth Brass Band as part of his research for our book. What struck him more than anything was the absorbing enthusiasm and happiness of the young people engaged in this now roughly 150-year-old tradition. As Harry Mortimer, marvellously happy and youthful at eighty-five, says: 'It can't be bad.'

A quick word is perhaps needed about the rather unorthodox structure of this book. We decided to base the book on a band programme from the past because it seemed appropriate and enabled us to diversify our chapters more than is usual. The solos are represented by interviews with four leading brass band figures: we chose a player, an administrator, a composer and a conductor in order to try to illustrate different aspects of the band world from personal viewpoints. The chapters dealing with the modern and traditional repertoires are not designed to be comprehensive but are, rather, my personal selection of some of the most

interesting and most important works. Similarly, our historical chapters only deal with major themes and personalities
(this book is not a history of brass bands; Arthur Taylor's
Brass Bands already covers that aspect of the subject
admirably). The final 'Chorus' we hope speaks for itself, and
provides an idea of how banding may change under the
influence of a new generation.

Perhaps we should end our overture with what seems to
be a necessary definition. Brass bands are still confused with
military bands, as they are known in the UK, or wind/
concert bands, to use the US term, both of which contain
woodwind instruments together with brass. They are further
confused with a more recent development, the modern brass
ensemble based on orchestral instruments; that is, trumpets,
orchestral (french) horns, trombones and tubas.

Oddly enough, the brass band never features the trumpet,
cornets being preferred as the leading soprano voice.
Neither do french horns have a place. The brass band is, in
fact, a consort of saxhorns, instruments developed by
Adolphe Sax (see p.18). The combination is fixed for
competition purposes as: one soprano cornet in E flat, four
solo cornets in B flat, five other B flat cornets (traditionally
one repiano[1], two seconds and two thirds), one flugel horn
in B flat, three tenor horns in E flat, two baritones in B flat,
two euphoniums in B flat, three trombones (two tenor, one
bass), two tubas in E flat and two contrabass tubas in BB
flat, plus two percussion players.

Elgar Howarth

---

1 'Repiano' is the brass band form of the term *ripieno* (supplementary)

2

Intermezzo

Early History

THE WORLD OF brass bands is one ruled by competitiveness. The desire to be better than one's peers is held by every true band, be they the 'cracks' (as they are known) of the Championship section or lesser bands who merely enter local contests. Yet rivalry does not stop here. Many bands fiercely contend that they are the original, the first, the oldest band in Britain. A number of bands can trace their origins back to the early nineteenth century, notables like Besses o' th' Barn and Black Dyke Mills among them, but none was in those days a truly brass band. To understand the brass bands' origins, therefore, we must first examine the history of their predecessors, the reed bands, and of the musicians who played in them.

Most students of brass bands cite three main musical traditions which by the beginning of the nineteenth century were in decline, and which it is believed may have evolved into wind or reed bands: the city waits, church bands, and the bands of the British Army. (In some respects these three traditions continue today as brass bands, Salvation Army bands and military bands, all distinctive in their make-up, music and activities.)

The most important of these three was probably the church bands, since they were the most widely spread. In 1644 the Puritans had issued an edict banning church organs; small wind and string ensembles replaced them as accompaniment for the Sunday service. Many of these groups also performed secular music at dances and other celebrations. In rural areas especially they had done much to keep a tradition of music-making alive. But as organs began to be widely reintroduced during the late eighteenth and early nineteenth centuries, the amount of work for church

14

musicians grew less, and many began to concentrate on secular music and to form themselves into string and reed bands. It should be pointed out that some areas do not fit into this simplified outline – some parishes never lost their organs, others kept their bands until the late nineteenth century – but it seems certain that many church bands declined at the turn of the century and that the musicians did look for new fields of performance.

Nowadays the term 'waits' conjures up pictures of carol singers who tour the streets at Christmas, often accompanied by brass bands, but before the nineteenth century the waits themselves were the instrumentalists. They had their origins in the Middle Ages, when they were watchmen who used musical instruments to raise the alarm or to herald the arrival of a distinguished visitor. In some cities they assembled into guilds and became municipal employees, but elsewhere they were ill-organized groups who performed irregularly at fairs, weddings and public festivals. However, the Municipal Corporation Act of 1835 (a time, interestingly, when many brass bands were getting started) officially put an end to these groups, although many had ceased to perform years before. Some of these unemployed musicians probably joined the growing number of new reed bands.

The other source of music, instrumentalists and, indeed, instruments was the army bands. The British Army had had bands during the Napoleonic Wars, and after the Battle of Waterloo many musicians returned home still eager to play; at the same time some instruments became available on the home market. But military influences were greater than these alone. Army music became an important source of repertoire – it is not surprising that the march is still the musical style most associated with brass bands, and uniforms have always been militaristic in fashion. Ties between army and civilian bands have remained strong, with each tradition providing the other with composers, conductors and players.

The merging of the waits and the church and army bands to appear as reed and wind bands in the nineteenth century is a shadowy metamorphosis – obviously not all the musicians went into the new groups; nor, by any means, were all the members of the new bands from one of these three traditions – but it does seem likely that the impetus behind the growth of the new ensembles owed its origins to a combination of the three influences.

Given that the origins of the reed bands are so obscure, it is a fruitless task to try to decide which brass band is the oldest, especially since much of the evidence is based on oral reminiscence. However, we can narrow the field a little, and this will have to suffice.

It is claimed that Besses o' th' Barn started life as a string band in the 1790s, becoming Clegg's Reed Band, named after the founders John, James and Joseph Clegg, cotton manufacturers, in 1818. By 1821 they had become Besses o' th' Barn, the name of an inn situated between Manchester and Bury where they rehearsed. According to the official history of the band, in the same year they won an impromptu local contest, one of the earliest recorded, with a crowd-pleasing rendition of 'God Save the King' at a procession to celebrate the Coronation of George IV.

Across the Pennines in Yorkshire, John Foster and Son Black Dyke Mills Band also have their origins in a pub and as a reed band. In 1816 Peter Wharton, publican of the Old Dolphin in Queenshead (now Queensbury), ran a small brass and reed band, one of whose members was a french horn player called John Foster. Wharton's band went into decline, but another village band replaced it in 1833. This group in turn declined in 1855, but was saved from extinction by the now wealthy John Foster, owner of Black Dyke Mill – it was to prove to have been well worth saving.

Stalybridge Old Band appeared in 1814 from the Hope and Anchor, Stalybridge, according to their centenary pamphlet. They played their first concert the following year, but, most interestingly, they travelled to Sheffield for a contest in 1818. Unfortunately we have no further information about this trip, but it is the earliest contest that we know about.

Two bands claim even earlier foundation than Stalybridge. New Mills Old Prize Band's centenary leaflet dates its beginnings to 1812, as a brass and reed band. However, a letter to the *Observer* in 1962 reported that the Coxlodge Band of the Burradon and Coxlodge Coal Company,

Durham, dated back to 1809, when a Mr Twiton and some employees founded an amateur band.

It should not be forgotten that all these bands were reed bands and that conversion to all-brass did not begin until the second quarter of the nineteenth century. The first band to re-equip itself is generally thought to have been Blaina Band from Monmouthshire. Blaina was subsidized by a local firm, Brown's Ironworks, whose commercial travellers brought over a set of the new valved brass instruments from Holland, probably in the early 1830s. This pattern proved to be typical.

The reed bands varied greatly in size, instrumentation and ability, but circumstances began to encourage growth, and were soon to promote a change to brass instruments. These circumstances were largely a result of the Industrial Revolution, which was developing apace during this period. Industrialization and urbanization had created a displaced workforce which had lost many of its traditional rustic entertainments. Agitation, radicalism and nonconformism had began to take a hold, and bands played their part in the increased political activity. The marchers to Peterloo in 1819 were led by their own bands; Stalybridge Old Band was fortunate to escape attack by the cavalry at St Peter's Fields, Manchester, in August 1819 – the band was warned of the approaching danger and slipped off home unharmed. Many people felt that working-class energies needed to be channelled into less dangerous pursuits, such as music. Employers began to finance works bands in order to keep the workforce off the streets – as John Foster was to realize, bands could also be a useful advertisement for the firm. Improved standards of musicianship were encouraged by the Mechanics' Institutes. Dr George Birkbeck had started the first in Glasgow in 1823 to help instruct a new breed of mechanic; they soon caught on and by 1860 there were about 750, mainly in the Midlands, Lancashire and Yorkshire (the first London Institute was later to become Birkbeck College, now part of the University of London). The Institutes also offered music classes, which the bandsmen and their conductors took advantage of in an insatiable desire to improve.

The Industrial Revolution had brought new technology, including new production skills in the manufacture of musical instruments. Better instruments meant better contest results, and soon every band wanted to change to an all-brass format.

The first of the new generation of instruments to appear was probably the cornopean, a prototype cornet from France. This was quickly adopted by the Coldstream Guards; indeed, it was professional ensembles – military or circus bands, for example – who spread the popularity of most new instruments. Wombwell's Circus Band was extremely popular in the North, and recruited many of its personnel from brass and reed bands. But the most influential professional groups were those led by Monsieur Jullien of Paris and John Distin of Devon.

M. Jullien first appeared in England in the 1830s, when he began a series of nationwide concert tours. His band of continental virtuosi was to have a lasting effect on Enderby Jackson, the great band entrepreneur of the 1850s and 1860s, who saw them perform in Hull. A later Jullien ensemble included the clarinettist John Gladney, who was to be the most successful contest conductor of the last three decades of the century.

Perhaps even more influential were John Distin and his four sons. This family quintet had begun touring in 1837 with only moderate success until, in 1844, they met Adolphe Sax in Paris. The Belgian instrument designer had recently brought his latest inventions to France – the saxhorn and the saxophone. At a concert to promote the two, organized by the composer Hector Berlioz, Distin was overwhelmed by the advance that they represented. He commissioned Sax to make a set of saxhorns of different sizes and pitches for his quintet, and immediately took them on tour. Wherever the Distins played, they received a rapturous reception, and their performance at the Great Exhibition of 1851 served to introduce the new instruments to an even wider public.

There has been only passing reference to contests so far, and as we are coming to the period when contesting became more organized and all-important, some background is necessary.

Contests are the lifeblood of the band world, providing a continuity of impetus which has been invaluable to the success of banding. Rivalry between bands has always been strong – challenges were thrown down long before formal contesting began. Nineteenth-century politicians often hired bands to enliven campaigns and challenges often ensued, though generally of a musical rather than a political nature. As we have seen, some bands use competitions to aid the dating of their foundation, such as the obscure Sheffield contest of 1818 at which Stalybridge Old Band was present. It is impossible to say why these competitions started, although natural rivalry must have played an important part. It could be that bands were not invited to established music festivals, such as the Eisteddfods of Wales, and so started their own. There is also evidence to suggest a French influence, because the famous Burton Constable contest of 1845 was the idea of 'the Ladies Chichester', who had witnessed band contests in the South of France. Whatever the origins, contests must have dramatically raised standards of musicianship and performance, and by the 1840s a thriving, if localized, contest circuit had grown up.

The contest at Burton Constable, near Hull, was probably no more than a rather grander local affair than was usual, because it was hosted by the lord of the manor, Sir Clifford Constable, as part of his Magdalen Day celebrations. Five bands competed, the eventual winners being James Walker's Wold Band. What makes this contest significant, though, is the presence of the eighteen-year-old Enderby Jackson, who never forgot his first experience of a brass band competition.

Six years later Jackson was in London for the Great Exhibition. Adolphe Sax was also there, displaying instruments, which were demonstrated to great effect by John Distin's quintet. At the exhibition Jackson met James Melling of Stalybridge and Tallis Trimnell of Chesterfield, both noted musicians and band enthusiasts. The three discussed brass band contests, but there the subject rested for some time.

One important feature of the Great Exhibition was the introduction of cheap railway travel for the working classes. By 1851 a complex and extensive railway network had been built, and workers were encouraged to come to London to bear witness to the power of Great Britain and to her manufacturing might. Radical politics had waned as a popular movement and there was no longer felt to be any danger to the state in large numbers of workers moving around the country – which twenty years earlier had been perceived as a real threat. The travel business was about to come into existence. The railway companies began to lay on excursions to the seaside and would soon be organizing special trains to the major brass band championships.

Enderby Jackson and James Melling went their separate ways after the Great Exhibition, but within a few years they had become rival contest promoters. Melling conducted the City Royal Brass Band at the Pomana Gardens, Manchester, but he also knew John Jennison, who in 1837 had opened the rival Belle Vue Zoological Gardens, among whose attractions by 1850 were 'three efficient brass bands'. The two joined forces in 1852 to promote a drum and fife band contest at Belle Vue, which was such a success that Jennison decided to add a brass band contest to his programme for 1853.

The first Belle Vue Championships were a chaotic triumph. Some of the special excursion trains were late, far more people turned up than had been expected (according to one estimate nearly 16,000 paying customers), the food ran out, and Mossley Temperance Saxhorn Band arrived late and had to play last – a bit of luck, as it happened, because they won; even today bands like to play as late in the draw as possible, although stricter rules prevent convenient tardiness. A massive firework display rounded off a splendid day, and Belle Vue seemed firmly established in the bandsman's calendar. In 1854 the entry increased to fourteen bands, six more than the year before, and attendance rose to 20,000. The following year featured fifteen bands and an important innovation, the first test-piece, 'Orynthia' by James Melling. Until now bands had always played an 'own-choice' selection in contests, but for the next twelve years they had to perform both their own work and a test-piece, the 'own-choice' selection finally being dropped in 1867. The Belle Vue Championships had got off to a good start, but as yet there was no rival event.

Later in his life Enderby Jackson complained that Melling and Jennison had stolen his idea; whether they had or not, they had certainly stolen his thunder. Jackson eventually staged his first contest in 1856 at the Zoological Gardens, Hull. He negotiated special low excursion fares with all the northern and Midlands railway companies and attracted a crowd of 14,000 to the event. Twenty-one bands entered but only twelve performed – presumably the other nine did not attend or were scared off by the standard of the opposition. Fittingly, the Band of the Railway Foundry (Leeds) were adjudged victors, with John Foster's recently revived Black Dyke Mills in second place. As at Belle Vue, each band played two pieces, an own-choice and the test-piece, Jackson's 'Yorkshire Waltzes'.

After this initial success Jackson began to promote contests around the country, often bringing bands to places where they were virtually unknown, such as Norwich. So popular were these events that they seem to have overshadowed the Belle Vue Championships, where entries fell at such an alarming rate that the 1859 contest had to be cancelled owing to lack of interest – only three bands entered. But Jackson had his sights set on even greater things. He had never forgotten the Great Exhibition and wanted to organize a brass band festival and competition in the capital.

Jackson wanted to use the Crystal Palace, which had been moved to Sydenham after the close of the exhibition, as the venue for his extravaganza, but the management wanted proof of his pulling-power before embarking on such a large-scale project. Therefore, in 1859, Jackson staged a handbell-ringing contest at the Palace. Twelve teams of ringers entered, many of which came from villages that also sent brass bands to Belle Vue and to Jackson's provincial competitions – proof of the variety of cultural activity in these areas. Although not a barnstorming success, Jackson had shown himself to be a capable promoter, and a brass band contest was announced for the following year.

Jackson decided to hold two separate contests on succeeding days, the 'great National Contest', an open competition, on the first day, and the 'Sydenham Amateur Contest', which would be open to all amateur bands who had won less than £20 prize-money during the previous year, on the second day. As eligible bands could enter both classes, it is difficult to know how many were present, since forty entered the 'National' and seventy the 'Sydenham' contest, but it was probably not many more than seventy bands. Over the weekend 27,000 people witnessed Black Dyke Mills win the 'National' and Cyfarthfa, from Crayshaw's Iron Works in South Wales, the 'Sydenham Amateur Contest'. A massed band performance, featuring over 1,200 musicians, according to *The Times*, was an additional attraction on the first day and the enthusiastic crowd demanded three encores. The festival had been extremely successful, both musically and financially, and the 1861 contests were equally so. But there seems to have been a diminution in interest the following year, when the event was scaled down to a single day. By 1863 the number of entries had dropped to forty-four, of which only twenty-one competed, and although the Crystal Palace advertised the contests as an annual event, 1863 was the last Crystal Palace competition for nearly forty years.

It seems that Jackson had become bored. He was unable to find a way of taking brass bands any further, and by the late 1860s had abandoned them totally; but his legacy was a rich one and was to inspire others to follow in his footsteps. The greatest loss was probably to the South of England, where the contests had fired much enthusiasm. A number of southern bands had performed creditably at Crystal Palace, and the London Victoria Amateurs had become the first band from the South to compete at Belle Vue, where they had been placed fifth – it would be many years before another southern group would do so well. Belle Vue seems to have been the only beneficiary from the demise of the London contests, because entries began to rise again in 1864 and crowds reached a record level of 25,000. Unchallenged, the Belle Vue Championships were to go from strength to strength in the next forty years.

Why did the contests become so popular so quickly? Apart from being a stage upon which to settle old rivalries and start new ones, the contests offered prizes of cash and new instruments. At a time when the average weekly wage was 24 shillings, few could afford to buy a new cornet, which cost 14 guineas. Yet the most successful bands were often those with the best instruments – Mossley Temperance Saxhorn Band, winners of the first Belle Vue contest in 1853, had been equipped with a brand-new set of saxhorns, supplied through John Distin. Many bands were changing to an all-brass instrumentation, and for some the only way they could get their hands on the necessary hardware was through contests. The prizes on the first day of the Crystal Palace festival of 1860 had been £40, a silver cup and a contrabass tuba, valued at 35 guineas, for the champions, with prizes of £25, £15, £10 and £5 respectively for the runners-up. Such rewards were obviously worth the winning, and there was reasonable prize-money available on the smaller local circuit, too. Even so, not all bands could be successful at contests and many must have been financially insecure – as we have seen, Black Dyke Mills were rescued from oblivion by the financial support of John Foster – but a new source of patronage appeared in the 1860s.

The Volunteer Movement began in 1859 to prepare the country for the possibility of invasion from France. Just as in the professional army, drill and marching were done to band music, so many bands volunteered their services. The corps were supported by industrialists and local landowners, who also subsidized the bands, often giving them rehearsal facilities, new instruments and uniforms. The importance of the movement to banding was immense. It saved some bands from extinction – the Bacup Band became the 4th Lancashire Rifle Volunteers (Bacup). It provided others with firm foundations – the Lewes Town Band began life as the Lewes Town and Volunteer Cinque Ports Band. It was also a training-ground for some important individuals – John Dennison, founder of the St Hilda Colliery Band, was a member of the 3rd Durham Artillery Volunteers; Charles Fry, founder of the first Salvation Army band, played first cornet in the 1st Wiltshire Volunteer Rifle Corps Band; Edwin Swift, soon to become one of banding's leading lights, was assistant conductor of Linthwaite Band in 1869 when it became the 3rd West Yorkshire Rifle Volunteers Band.

Both before the Volunteer Movement and after its demise, some bands had enjoyed another form of patronage. John Foster and Sons provided Black Dyke with financial support and the bandsmen with jobs; in return, as the band became successful, Foster obtained useful advertising for his firm. The loss of managerial support could have catastrophic results – the great Meltham Mills Band collapsed while at the height of its powers in the 1880s because the mill withdrew its money. Some bands, on the other hand, had to fend for themselves. These were the 'subscription bands', such as Besses o' th' Barn. Their initial finance was provided by the members themselves or by subscriptions from supporters. Contest prize-money and concert engagements were their only other sources of income, apart from the occasional gift of cash from a wealthy local patron. Many bands today have to finance themselves by using similar traditional methods, such as playing carols at Christmas or performing at fêtes in the summer.

A new sphere of activity grew up in the 1870s which led to an increase in popularity and financial stability. Many people's mental picture of a brass band would be of one performing on a bandstand in the local park on Sunday or at the seaside in summer. Once again the railways played an important role; cheap excursion fares encouraged people to go to the sea, where brass bands were one of the main attractions. The first band to be invited to perform at a resort was the Leeds Temperance Band, who were paid £60 for a four-week engagement at Scarborough in 1847 – it was so successful that they were invited back for the next two years. This was a very early experiment, however, for it was not until the last quarter of the nineteenth century that working-class holidays, and the band entertainments which accompanied them, became widely popular. During the same period park concerts were introduced. In a time of limited leisure and literacy the pub and the pleasure garden were the main sources of entertainment in towns. Band concerts were almost the only opportunities many people had of hearing operatic music or the work of new composers or old classical favourites. The bands that performed such works enjoyed the height of their popularity during this period, before the growth of alternative entertainments in the twentieth century began to deprive them of their audience.

The years from 1870 to the end of the century were the great years for brass banding, when popularity reached a peak, when a number of bands established themselves as the best, or the 'cracks', and when contesting was further formalized and securely established. This increased popular support could lead to trouble, however, with some bands acquiring a tarnished reputation. The *British Bandsman*'s reports of the Belle Vue Championships of September 1888 tell us that the judges were hissed and booed; furthermore, only police protection prevented a physical assault on the adjudicators as they tried to leave the hall. Earlier in the year one Dr Spark had ajudicated at a contest at Barnold-swick near Skipton. His final decision was very unpopular with a section of the crowd, and only the protection of Leeds Forge Band, whom he had placed second, saved him from attack by the lower-placed bands and their followers during the rail journey home. Today adjudicators' decisions may still rarely be universally popular, but thankfully the judges no longer live in fear of assault.

While bands were attracting larger audiences on bandstands and contest stages, the number of bands was steadily increasing. Banding was becoming big business. New instruments were being designed and produced, and by the mid-1890s the band world was healthy enough to support fifty-two firms of brass instrument manufacturers. Further proof of this widespread activity was the first meeting of the British Amateur Band Association in Manchester in 1893. The twenty-two bands present passed four resolutions: that each band should submit a membership list to the Association; that no bandsman should register with more than one band; that only Association-approved adjudicators should be used; and that for contest purposes no band should consist of more than twenty-four musicians. A few miles away in Wigan the Lancashire Brass Band Association was holding its inaugural meeting, and was reaching very much the same conclusions. But despite all this activity a national band association was never founded; indeed, the idea is still looked upon with mistrust, and it has largely been left to the regional organizations to look after banding in their own areas.

It was also during this period, the latter half of the nineteenth century, that publishers began to show an interest in brass banding; as the number of bands increased, so a new market for sheet music and periodicals was created. The first publisher of brass band music was Richard Smith, the great Yorkshire band trainer and conductor, who had won at Belle Vue in 1854 and at Enderby Jackson's contest in Hull in 1856, on both occasions conducting the Leeds Railway Foundry Band. Smith published his *Champion Brass Band Journal* for the first time in 1857; up until that time bandsmen had used music from circus bands or, like Peter Wharton, founder of the Queenshead band, military band scores. In 1878 Smith moved his operations from Hull to London, where he died in 1890, leaving the editorship of the journal to Samuel Cope, founder of the *British Bandsman*.

Three years before Smith's move to London, Harry Round and Thomas Wright had started a publishing company in Liverpool. Apart from producing new arrangements and compositions, in 1881 Wright and Round began to publish the first paper exclusively devoted to brass bands and their activities. Six years later Samuel Cope, a composer and arranger, founded his own magazine in London, the *British Bandsman*. Both papers commented on a thriving banding scene, in particular showing the supremacy of the Belle Vue Championships over all other contests.

After a few lean years Belle Vue had recovered from the threat posed by Enderby Jackson's rival promotions, and it had grown to be regarded as the supreme championship. So popular had the contest in September become that the organizers introduced a July contest for bands who had not won a prize during the previous four years, with the winner being invited to the main championship a few months later. Although audiences were not as large as in September, the new contest was deemed successful enough to continue and soon became a regular fixture in the banding calendar.

New contesting regulations were laid down at Belle Vue in 1889, primarily to combat the problem of professionalism. The most successful, and therefore often the richest, bands had begun to hire professional soloists, usually cornet soloists, to add that competition-winning extra sparkle on the big day. The best-known example is that of Alexander Owen, who was hired by Meltham Mills purely to play the cornet for them on important occasions – during his stay there the band won a hat-trick of victories at Belle Vue between 1876 and 1878. After 1889 every performer had to earn his chief income outside music; except, that is, for conductors, who could be professional musicians and could conduct as many bands as would hire them.

However, the real story of Belle Vue during the years 1860–1900 is that of the bands who competed there and of the conductors who led them, for it was at this time that the band world acquired its first stars. The Bacup 4th Lancashire Rifle Volunteers dominated the first decade of this period, winning four times and being placed as many again, before somewhat abruptly ceasing to function in 1871. Bacup's superiority was soon assumed by Meltham Mills Band and their conductor John Gladney, who won four times in six years between 1873 and 1878. This was the beginning of a quite remarkable run of victories for Gladney, who soon established himself as the dominant figure of the end of the century.

John Gladney was born in Belfast in 1839, where he received a good musical education. He had performed with M. Jullien and with various northern groups, and played the clarinet in the Hallé Orchestra from 1860 onwards. But he also had brass band roots, for his father had been a military bandmaster and John himself had conducted a Volunteer Band in Burnley. After the collapse of Meltham Mills Band in the 1880s, Gladney conducted many bands in many contests – as the rules allowed – winning at Belle Vue eleven times between 1884 and the turn of the century.

His closest rivals were Alexander Owen and Edwin Swift. Edwin Swift was a virtually self-taught musician; an accomplished flautist, he taught himself musical theory, harmony

and arranging while working at the mill in his home town of
Linthwaite, near Huddersfield. He was assistant conductor
of the town band when they became the 3rd West Yorkshire
Rifle Volunteers in 1869, a year in which they were also
placed fifth at Belle Vue. Five years later, with Swift
conducting, Linthwaite won the title. This success enabled
Edwin to leave the mill and concentrate on his music – in the
next decade he tasted success with Littleborough Public
Band and Wyke Temperance.

Alexander Owen had been professional solo cornet at
Meltham Mills Band in the 1870s, but, while there, had
already started conducting and training bands. In 1879 he
was appointed to Black Dyke, who had won at Belle Vue
that year under another man. Owen completed a hat-trick
for them in 1880 and 1881 and a personal hat-trick, with
Clayton-le-Moors, in 1882.

Gladney, Swift and Owen dominated band conducting for
thirty years. They had all the best bands and therefore
virtually always won – for example, in 1882 they each
conducted two of the top bands at Belle Vue. But it was not
just at Belle Vue that they were dominant, for each of them
was a talented composer-arranger, and so they also trium-
phed at other contests where the 'own-choice' selection was
still in operation. This self-sufficiency of band and conductor
was to become common once again in the later part of the
new century, and it is fitting that the era of these three giants
should pave the way to brass banding in the twentieth
century.

3

Cornet Solo

A Player: Bram Gay

BRAM GAY is from South Wales, where at an early age he became a cornet soloist with the Salvation Army. Later he received lessons from the celebrated bandsman Harry Mortimer, whose place he was to take in the famous Foden's Motor Works Band, which was conducted by Harry's father Fred Mortimer and also featured Harry's younger brothers Alex and Rex. After National Service Bram Gay joined the City of Birmingham Symphony Orchestra as principal trumpet. From there he moved to the Hallé Orchestra and, finally, to the Royal Opera House, Covent Garden. In 1971, through his involvement with the music publishers Novello, he and television producer Arthur Taylor founded the Granada Television Band of the Year Contest, in which bands perform half-hour 'own-choice' programmes rather than the traditional test-piece. He is now Orchestra Director at Covent Garden, where Patrick Howarth talked to him in January 1987.

PATRICK HOWARTH: *You came from a Salvation Army background, didn't you?*

BRAM GAY: Yes. My background was exactly like your father's, I think, except that I probably wasn't as well taught.

PATRICK HOWARTH: *Who did teach you?*

BRAM GAY: My father tried, but he couldn't. Like trying to teach your wife to drive, it always ends in tears! My father was a coalminer, as was his father. I suppose I am the classic example of the working-class boy taught music *in* the Salvation Army, rather than because of the Salvation Army.

I was given a cornet when I was about three, in case I could do something with it. When I was six it was thought that I should be taught properly, so my father tried, but couldn't. My mother was one of ten kids – seven brothers all played in a Salvation Army band, and some of them were very, very good.

PATRICK HOWARTH: *Where was this?*

BRAM GAY: The Rhondda Valley in Wales. Some of my mother's family were very gifted, and she'd seen them play, and knew how to do it, she thought. She showed me how to make a noise on this thing. I remember distinctly that I'd be crawling with a cornet in my hand, and she'd say: 'Go on, make a noise like a moo-cow for me.' I went on making a noise like a moo-cow for thirty or forty years after.

My production was quite wrong. I learnt badly accidentally. I fought against it all my playing life, and to this day if I pick up a cornet I blow it with a mistaken embouchure. Nobody spotted it until it was too late to change it without causing absolute havoc. Harry Mortimer saw it and did nothing. Ernie Hall[1] saw it, pondered and did nothing. I was playing first trumpet by then, and so carried on in the same way. I always said that when I stopped playing professionally I would start again properly. I still think I'll do that – it would be very interesting. I think I'll either play very much better than I did before, or not at all.

1 The late Ernest Hall was principal trumpet player with the London Symphony Orchestra and the BBC Symphony Orchestra, and a renowned teacher.

PATRICK HOWARTH: *What age were you when you joined the Salvation Army band?*

BRAM GAY: I was six and a half. I was auditioned in my grandmother's kitchen by the junior bandmaster, Harold Nash's[2] father. I played a hymn tune called 'Rimington', which was No 23 in the Salvation Army hymn book, twice through and he let me in.

The earliest memory I have of any major event was after the abdication of the poor old Duke of Windsor. It was necessary for the new King to become widely popular before his Coronation, and there was a great youth rally in Cardiff Arms Park in which nearly every youth organization in South Wales took part, including our junior band. I remember being seven and marching around the streets of Cardiff trying to play the cornet – I hadn't the legs to march or the lungs to blow. But I remember getting to Cardiff Arms Park and seeing the new King and Queen and the two little girls. I was the tiniest tot on parade and the Queen (the Queen Mother, as she is now) patted me on the head. That is my earliest memory of playing the cornet in public.

PATRICK HOWARTH: *Did you ever have any formal lessons?*

BRAM GAY: My father continued to try to teach me until I was ten, when I was sent to the then conductor of the Cory Band, Reginald Little, a Midlands and Northern bandsman expatriate, working at the top of a coal mine on a weighing-machine so that he could conduct the Cory Band. He was a very, very fine teacher. He taught half a

2 Principal trombone player at the Royal Opera House, Covent Garden.

dozen people who subsequently became corner-men[1] in very good bands in England. He also taught Harold Nash the trombone, and the great Emlyn Bryant the soprano cornet. You may not have heard of Emlyn, but he was a soprano cornet genius of the most astonishing kind. If Emlyn had only been managed properly, he would have been the most brilliant Bach trumpet player that God ever put on this planet. He would have had no difficulty with the Brandenburg [Concerto No 2] in musicality or style, even on a B flat instrument.

At that time I became a bit of a celebrity, playing cornet solos with the Salvation Army. I'll tell you what that's like – you tear to the other end of the land on Saturday to play Saturday-night festivals and all day on Sunday, and tear all the way back on Sunday night to try to get to school on Monday. It's not much fun, nor is it very good for you, although it does give you tremendous self-possession in front of an audience.

I remember seeing your father doing the same sort of thing, playing in Wolverhampton. I'm sure he won't mind my saying so, but I wasn't very impressed with his cornet playing. If anyone had told me then that he would go on to play the trumpet as well as he did, I would never have believed them. Someone took a very big grip on him at the Royal Manchester College, because, believe me, that was a trumpet player and three-quarters! At that

---

1 Traditionally the chief soloists of a band, comprising the solo cornet, solo tenor horn, solo euphonium and solo trombone; today the flugel horn and soprano cornet can also be regarded as such.

time I was a much better cornet player than he was, but I never thought that I could have competed with him as a trumpet player afterwards.

My next teaching, however, was from Harry Mortimer, and that was teaching of a very different kind.

PATRICK HOWARTH: *Was this when you joined Foden's?*

BRAM GAY: Yes. In 1943 I was taken to play to Harry simply because my father didn't know what to do with me.

PATRICK HOWARTH: Was that a big break, going from the Salvation Army to a secular brass band like Foden's?

BRAM GAY: Oh, yes, indeed. It was a tremendous upheaval for a boy of thirteen, especially one who had been brought up to believe that the Salvation Army was the only place to play. Then suddenly there was this complete turnaround on the part of my parents, simply because they had taken me to see Harry, who thought I was quite important. They were so impressed with him, I think, that they could see no let or hindrance as to why I should not give up playing with the Salvation Army. I continued to play as a soloist with the Salvation Army for a long time after that, but it made life very uncomfortable for me.

PATRICK HOWARTH: *Had the religious aspects of the Salvation Army been important to you and your family?*

BRAM GAY: Well, your religious attitudes are those fed to you with your mother's milk, until you're old enough to think for yourself. The Salvation Army has one big inbuilt snag – I've said this many times: you don't christen a child in the Salvation Army, a child is dedicated to God *and* the Salvation Army. A child who goes to church, just goes to church, whereas a child who is in the Salvation Army and a Salvation Army band, goes to the Salvation Army to play in a band. I'm not trying to convince you that this is universally so. I know many Salvation Army members who are Christians first, Salvationists next, and bandsmen after that. But I think that, with a child, there is a risk of this attitude. Certainly I was a bandsman first, and the religious side was a background to the banding; I think this must be true of many Salvation Army children.

PATRICK HOWARTH: *So by the time you were thirteen the Salvation Army was, in many respects, behind you?*

BRAM GAY: Yes. I remember I was taken to Belle Vue, where Harry was adjudicating the May contests, and I met him in the green-room before he went into the judges' box. I played Handel's 'I know that my Redeemer liveth' from somebody's solo album. He then produced his own solo album, published by Boosey and Hawkes, and made me play the Waltz Song from Gounod's *Romeo and Juliet,* to see if I could. I thought it was rather a good tune. He then took out his cornet, and said: 'Do you think you could play it like this?' I'd never heard a sound from a cornet like it. Nothing so easy, so beautiful, so absolutely musical ever came out of a brass instrument as what that man could do with a simple tune. I was fascinated. And I found that I could in fact, using my very primitive, instinctive technique, copy

Mortimer with enormous success. I became an instant Mortimer copy, which was very dangerous – that wasn't teaching. It's a moot point whether it was a good thing or not, but I could do it, so I was immediately taken off to Foden's and put on repiano cornet at the back.

PATRICK HOWARTH: *What was Foden's band like at that time?*

BRAM GAY: They had an incredible soprano cornet, I remember – Charlie Cook, one of the greatest brass players I ever heard. Not an Emlyn Bryant, but a subtle musician who could play octaves like an organ stop over the solo cornet. On the other side of me was the great Hubert Shergold, who made the only true flugel sound I've ever heard in my life. No one plays like that today; it's all wide and diffuse, wide-bore and fluffy. Hubert had a kind of super-cornet noise, very broad and sweet, but very centred. That band knew the brass band repertoire. It was the most incredible place to take a child to play. You had Harry Mortimer playing solo cornet, Alex Mortimer playing solo euphonium ... you had basically the band that had won at Crystal Palace ten years earlier, and they had been together for ten years before that. The horn section had been together for twenty-eight years. The newest recruit was Charlie Cook, who had joined in 1932, and they thought he was quite a raw recruit, really. It was an incredible honour to be there.

PATRICK HOWARTH: *It must have been a very overpowering experience for a thirteen-year-old?*

BRAM GAY: Oh, yes. They were getting older; there was hardly anyone in it who wasn't old enough to have been my father. It was a very strange atmosphere for a boy of thirteen. We were so busy, always playing. There was a broadcast once every two weeks – a lot of bands were on the radio in those days, not like now; our turn came round once a fortnight simply because we could play all the pieces. A band programme was half an hour long, and we had this amazing habit of running up to Manchester on a Friday night and playing three original brass band masterpieces which we had prepared between Monday and Thursday. We didn't know what they would be, nor did we much care, because the band had them in their heads. We would sit down on a Monday night and there was Percy Fletcher's 'Epic Symphony', for instance. I was the only person in the band who couldn't whistle them. I was reading like mad; it was a terrible musical stretch for me. But it wasn't only their own pieces – they could knock off things like 'On the Cornish Coast' by Henry Geehl, which was a St Hilda's test-piece from ten years before Foden's really surfaced. They still had that repertoire, though. It was all there – all the obscure pieces by Denis Wright; and as for the ancient operatic selections, they were just basic – [William] Rimmer's works or Alex Owen's 'Rossini's Works', although some of the soloists had to fight for the cadenzas because the band had long since lost that knack. But as far as the music was concerned, the band was absolute dynamite. It was the most extraordinary crash-course in musical education for seven years. The value decreased, I suppose, with the shock value. I used to be afraid to go to band practice because I had no idea what was going to hit me.

They all thought it was rather funny, I think.

PATRICK HOWARTH: *You were presumably still at school while doing all this?*

BRAM GAY: I used to have to travel to band practice, sixty miles each way. School was very good to me; they realised I was never going to do any work. I was simply not missed when I wasn't there – registers were fiddled and so on to make sure I wasn't disturbed. They thought they were being very good, but in retrospect I know they were very silly; they should have tied me down and made me learn a language or two. But at the time I was thrilled. I enjoyed playing enormously, except that I was under tremendous pressure. I wouldn't do it to a child, especially since the great man's tactics, Fred Mortimer's tactics, were to overreact to my situation. As a father he could see the awful danger to a teenager of that atmosphere. Not that they were badly behaved chaps; they weren't. They were a very disciplined band. It was more than that – they were nice people, they were a family.

PATRICK HOWARTH: *Will you tell me something of Fred Mortimer?*

BRAM GAY: A genius, you know. An absolute, natural genius. Sir Adrian Boult once said that the amateur brass band was the best example of the innate musicality of the British. If that is the case, then Fred Mortimer was the absolute apogee of that musicality. He knew nothing at all about music, in the sense that I think I do, or your father thinks he does, yet he had the whole thing wrapped up. He was a natural conducting and teaching artist, who had all the right instincts. I've never heard anything he expounded to me bruised, never mind contradicted, by any good artist I've worked with since. He worked simply on the basis that the score was the imperishable truth and not to be tampered with. If the work wasn't good enough, you didn't play it at all; but if it was good enough, then you played it with absolute fidelity. He didn't interpret, but he did what all the great interpeters do: he tried to give an honest account of what he saw before him and what he heard. By the time he'd finished doing that, there was no room left for distortion, which is what usually passes for interpretation. He came out with something totally original and unlike anybody else's, because he had never thought how he was going to do it.

PATRICK HOWARTH: *He was known as a tough disciplinarian.*

BRAM GAY: He was enormously tough, a natural disciplinarian, but he wasn't a bully. Conversation stopped when he came in, and that was that. A marvellous natural leader of men. He was only a little chap, you know, and not at all presumptuous, just an ordinary, pipe-smoking, bank manager type. There was no great side to him, but he was not a man to be trifled with at all. He was original Yorkshire of the best sort. If you crossed Fred Mortimer, you crossed him for life; if he lost confidence in you, you never won him back. Things were absolute with Fred: you were either right or wrong, either trustworthy or a bank-robber. A ha'penny was a ha'penny, and if you did Fred out of a ha'penny, he'd never trust you with anything again. His musical

values were the same – you were either
playing flat out or you weren't, and if you
weren't he didn't want to know about you.
I must say the band always pretended to
treat him, in conversation, as if he were
some sort of joke. Because the band had
been formed by Mr Rimmer and trained
by Mr Halliwell,[1] Fred had had it all his
own way and was a very lucky man – this is
how the old hands treated it. In fact it was
nothing of the kind, of course. They knew
perfectly well what a treasure they'd got.
The proof of that came before he died,
when he was too ill to conduct, and Harry
was brought in. They made it very clear,
politely, that he was but a learner and not
be treated seriously, like Dad. Harry tried
to conduct, but nothing ever changed. Of
course, Harry was a conductor; the old
man just let the band play. Harry made
demands, gave instructions, but they were
as water off a duck's back. He could work
all day to impose a bit of HM on something they'd been doing for twenty years
with the old man, but nothing ever
changed.

PATRICK HOWARTH: *So Harry was very different from his
father, was he?*

BRAM GAY: Oh, totally different. I'd played next to
Harry for a little while before he left me to
it, and that's when my troubles really
began, because that was when I really had
to play. The old man gave me hell ...

PATRICK HOWARTH: *How old were you by then?*

BRAM GAY: Fifteen.

---

1 See pp. 66–7

PATRICK HOWARTH: *So you'd worked your way up to solo cornet in about two years?*

BRAM GAY: Yes. I was repiano cornet for about one year; then I went to sit next to Harry, because the band knew he wasn't going to last. He didn't want to, though. He shouldn't have given up when he did; he could have gone on for another ten years at least. He was in terrific form when he stopped.

PATRICK HOWARTH: *So you had been brought in specifically to replace Harry Mortimer?*

BRAM GAY: They could see no other alternative. To the day I left that band I hadn't enough technique for it. I hadn't done enough study of the instrument or methodical work at the technique; I did all that in the army. I was never a replacement for Harry. Don't let anyone tell you I was. It was a marvellous con-trick. The sound was the same, in a kind of sixty-five per cent way. The range was never as great, the technique was never as great, the command was never as great and I could never play tunes like that; I could play like some kind of pale reflection of that man but . . .

I was really put through the mill, even by Harry, because his way of teaching was: 'Do it like me.' That happened in lessons – he'd watch me do it and say, 'Well, you're saying it like this and I'm saying it like that. Can you say it like that?' And I could; but then we'd get into the concert hall. In those days we used to do a lot of arrangements, stuff like Sullivan which was terribly good for cornet players. We'd play something like 'Take a pair of sparkling eyes' which had a repeat. Now normally a band wouldn't do the repeat – it wasn't an important enough piece, it was only in there for the old ladies – but when I sat next to Harry we would play the repeat. Whereas in lessons I did it first, then he showed me, then I repeated, in band concerts this was not the case: I was made to play the first time, always, and by the time we'd reached the first time bar I'd be convinced that I'd done rather well, and so would all the old ladies. Then would come the repeat and I'd get a total put-down of what I'd just played. I imagine it was good for me, but it left permanent scars.

PATRICK HOWARTH: *It sounds like a very tough way of learning the ropes.*

BRAM GAY: It was tough, terribly tough. The old man was even worse in band practices. You'd deliver some really impressive display at 9.25pm, just before the end of practice, and think to yourself: 'I've really been solo cornet tonight.' As he closed the score he'd say to himself, but just loud enough for me to hear: 'Well, thank you very much. It's a marvellous piece – glad you enjoy it.' But as he was going out he would add: 'Of course, to play a piece like that you have to have a cornet player like our 'Arry.' The strange thing was, as I found out years later when talking to Harry (because I know him very much better now, although he still thinks I'm thirteen!), that Fred never let Harry believe he was a good player. I don't know if it was as severe as the treatment I got, but it may have been because he was dealing with his son. However, when I told Harry about that remark, he was absolutely stunned, because he had ncver been allowed to know that his father thought him a good player. Never. And that is rather a pity, because he was without any doubt, in terms of a player who leads the brass band, head and shoulders above any other player who ever lived. He was a tremendous artist. In the way the great violinists of the world lead the great orchestras, Harry led bands. His turn of phrase infected everybody; the attack came from him and nobody else; the lack of attack, when required, came from him as well. Everything about it was so beautifully done. It came, he said, from watching Fritz Kreisler and the best singers in the world in his Hallé days. He thought that you couldn't learn how to be a musician from being in a brass band; you had to go out and watch great artists playing, singing and conducting.

PATRICK HOWARTH: *Do you agree?*

BRAM GAY: Oh, yes, absolutely. I don't want to put banding down, but if you wish to be a first-rate artist you must hear first-rate artists, watch how they react to the music, to stimulus, and to people; you have to be moved by listening to a great soprano singer before you know anything about phrasing. As Ernest Hall once said to me: 'Bruno Walter taught me how to play the trumpet, no one else. He taught me what a phrase should sound like, how I could sing with the instrument. Until I played *The Ring* for Bruno Walter I knew nothing about music.' That is the sort of education Harry had from Harty and Beecham. He talks about Beecham as if he was the greatest conductor – Harry always wanted to conduct like Beecham. Having watched Harry over many years, I can say that, Carlos Kleiber apart, I do not know of a conductor better at communicating with his hands than Mortimer. Had he been given the break that other people have been given, we might have had another Beecham, or another Barbirolli – at least a great British conductor. He is probably the greatest British conductor we never had. It's a tragedy.

PATRICK HOWARTH: *Did he ever conduct orchestrally?*

BRAM GAY: Yes, he conducted a concert with the Birmingham Symphony Orchestra once, which I played in. He walked into that, did all the right things with his hands, and we played beautifully. He had three hours' rehearsal for a two-hour concert, and had no trouble at all commanding precision, attack or organization from the orchestra. He's terribly good.

He was very different from his father, though. Harry was a pro – he said: 'Watch the beat.' This professional approach enabled him to conduct three bands a day and win four out of five prizes at the Albert Hall with any good bands. The old man wasn't like that; he couldn't conduct any old band in any old piece. He had an incredible chamber group around him which understood all about it – if he just advertised a fault he didn't have to correct it, the band corrected it for themselves. Rubato, for example, was played within certain received limits, as dictated by the old man, but was actually arranged by players between themselves. If you had a little phrase in an operatic piece where the soprano and the tenor were singing a cadenza together, the stick went down and you looked across the band to the first baritone who was playing with you, you played together, and then the band would pop up again at the end of it. In fact, music, that's what it was all about. Fred was a very, very good teacher; I was very lucky to be there. I learnt more music from Fred Mortimer than from any other person in my life.

PATRICK HOWARTH: *When you went to Birmingham did you continue your involvement with bands?*

BRAM GAY: While I was at Birmingham I had a little band called the John Thompson Works Band, in Wolverhampton, which had not won a prize for twenty-nine years. It was in the fourth section of the National Championships, and within four years it was in the first section – that's when the luck ran out.

In the National, indeed in any major brass band contest, it is true that all the bands below the top section are very bad, or very good, depending on how you look at it. They are all very much of a muchness. All you have to do is get them in tune, make them play together, get some essential musicality into it, and you are bound to win, you cannot fail. Therefore it was quite inevitable, and no particular credit to me, that I should win in the third section and the second section. But when you get to the first section you meet the brick wall, because they can actually play properly, and you need the players to do that. At that point you cannot actually push them hard enough, so you get stuck. Not that I think winning contests is all that important; it isn't really to me. I've never had the kind of blood-lust it takes. I'm not at all competitive, you know – actually I'm a bad loser, basically a coward. It's funny, I wasn't a coward with a trumpet in my hands. I was very nervous, but it never showed. As far as conducting a band goes, however, it's not that I mind being beaten, it's that I expect to be. That is probably unfair to the band. Winning is what counts to them.

Fortunately I went to the Hallé soon after that, and in Manchester I did a bit, but not very much. Again it was with lower-section bands like Blackly and Whitworth. That band was great fun; they were tremendous sports. We used to knock off the regionals in great style, with selections from *Scheherazade,* that sort of stuff. I remember a gentleman of eighty years of age who played the cornet – he was God's gift to the cornet, made a gorgeous great fat noise on it. He got married a few years later and died shortly afterwards! But I didn't have too much involvement until I came to Covent Garden. I still had the itch, what Harry Mortimer calls 'stick itch' – 'Every solo cornet player has stick itch,' he says. He always said I had no conducting talent at all; now he says I have, and he tries to find me opportunities to conduct.

I went to the Cory Band for two years. They had won the National and blown up; they were in a mess, and since it was my home-town band I went to help them. It's a funny thing with bands, but if you win the National with an outsider – as Cory were then, and as I suppose they are again now – through real conducting genius like Arthur Kenney's, but with no real muscle to sustain it, you always blow up. Harry Mortimer said that when the Luton Band won in 1929, with him on the cornet, his father training them, and Halliwell conducting, it was the worst thing that could have happened to them. They were getting seconds and thirds and were quite happy with that. But when you become National Champions everyone wants you to play and you don't have the repertoire, you don't have the muscle or the stamina, you don't have the mental reserves to carry it, and the band collapses. Also people leave – people who have been working with a band for ten years, or twenty years even, to push it to the top, night after night, week after week; at the age of forty-five or fifty they win, they've done it and it's over, for them. At Cory there were ten changes in the band. I went down and spent two years basically rebuilding it, which is probably what I'm good at. I think I'm a better teacher and trainer than I am a performer, perhaps.

Conducting is not a thing that a player can just do; I know players have done it, but few actually make it and develop into really top-class conductors. Hans Richter did it, Toscanini, Barbirolli, so I suppose there are a few. It's the same in bands – cornet players pick up the stick, but they are rarely real conductors. Conducting is an art that cannot be taught from nothing; you must have a certain natural aptitude for it, but, having got that, it is essential to study it seriously. Although I didn't really fail at Cory – we picked up a fourth at Belle Vue and a sixth and a seventh at the Albert Hall, which is respectable – nor did

I really succeed, and I don't expect to be involved with conducting bands again.

PATRICK HOWARTH: *At what point did you begin to set up the Granada Contest?*

BRAM GAY: That was quite early on, before I went into management here at Covent Garden. Granada took over Novello Publishing and, like everyone else at Novello's, I was given a circular asking me to inform Lord Bernstein of any ways in which the company could benefit from the Granada group and in which Granada could benefit from its association with us. So I wrote a thesis on what Novello could do for bands through Granada, some of which was followed through – although, in my view, some of the wrong things.

PATRICK HOWARTH: *What ideas do you feel were wasted?*

BRAM GAY: We never developed the publishing side to the extent that we should. We never involved ourselves in the promotion of concerts, which I think is important, because it is only in concerts that you can get what you want played by people you want and the conductor you want. We never went into instrument sales, which was a natural for Granada in my opinion. We did go in for magazine publishing, although I said we shouldn't, and did that terribly well. *Sounding Brass* was a very entertaining magazine, and a lot of fun to do, but we were not prepared to sustain it past the point where the economics became dangerous. Somebody said to me at a meeting of the National Association of Brass Band Conductors, 'Who is going to read this magazine, Bram?' I replied:

'Gentlemen, our magazine is for the thinking bandsman', and the chairman said
'Abandon hope – there aren't any!' I know
what he meant now, and essentially he was
right: there weren't enough to pay for a
quality magazine, that's for sure. It stag-
gered along for seven or eight years until
the company decided they couldn't afford
it any more. We found someone to take it
over, painlessly, but they did it appallingly
badly and it died. The new publishers had
their own input, wanted it to go a certain
way, the editors resigned and subscribers
stopped buying it. Over the years we had
developed a readership in tune with what
we were thinking, but it wasn't large
enough to pay for the magazine. The new
publishers changed the format to attract
new readers, and in doing so lost the old
readership. So it died, which is rather a
pity.

One of the things I did say to Granada,
however, was: 'I suppose we must have a
band contest. I am not in favour of band
contests, I do not like band contests, but I
suppose we must have one if we are to be
involved with brass bands.'

PATRICK HOWARTH: *Do you think the Granada Contest has
                        changed banding at all?*

BRAM GAY: Yes.

PATRICK HOWARTH: *For better or worse?*

BRAM GAY: Only time will tell. It would have been
                        easier for Granada to buy either the
                        National or the [Belle Vue] Open, but I
                        thought that if we were going to do this,
                        then we should have a bit of a stir, so we
                        set up the format we now have. It took me
                        a year to persuade the bands that it was a

credible thing to do, and sometimes they still wonder about it. I think it's a fairly hairy sort of day – anyone can win it, anything can happen. In some ways it doesn't matter who wins; Granada is just a big exhibition of what the best bands are doing. It's the only time in the year when the best bands get together to listen to what one another are doing, so it's valuable in that way. I'm disappointed with it now – we need some new ideas. The only development I can see for it is European involvement; I could see it becoming a European championship, with Eurovision exposure.[1]

PATRICK HOWARTH: *Is Granada interested in this idea?*

BRAM GAY: Yes, vaguely; but no one's making any decisions about it at the moment. The only problem, in my view, is that knowing the European banding scene as I do, it might well assume far greater importance in their eyes than the present European Brass Band Championship. Although I don't want to undermine what someone else is doing, if I'm given the challenge then I won't be able to resist it.

PATRICK HOWARTH: *Is European banding more geared to a Granada-style competition?*

BRAM GAY: It is more geared to an open mind.

PATRICK HOWARTH: *How involved are you on the Continent?*

BRAM GAY: I go twice a year to Sweden, and in fact I seem to conduct well there. I get very good playing from Swedish bands. I get all the time and attention I need – they seem to

1 The 1987 Granada Band of the Year Contest on the Isle of Man included a band from Holland.

be interested in those aspects of the music which interest me, so I don't bore them.

In the first year of Granada everyone had the wrong ideas, except Cory, who had won a television contest a few weeks before and had learnt a lot from it, so they won. They came in when Black Dyke opted out a week before the contest – for Cory to win at such short notice was wonderful. The following year your father arrived and demonstrated precisely what was required, and ever since then they have all been doing it. Occasionally he still turns up and throws a spanner in the works, like the conductorless band last year, but that wasn't really a musical contribution. It shook everyone rigid, but all we learnt there was that Grimethorpe can play like a clock. What is really needed is for someone to come along every three or four years and present something as original as your father's original input.

PATRICK HOWARTH: *And you think European involvement might provide this impetus?*

BRAM GAY: Yes, I do, actually. I think the continental bands will do it very badly to start with, but they will get there in the end. It would be a long time before they won it, perhaps, because you have got to be able to play well. You can't think yourself into it, or compose or arrange yourself into it; you're at the mercy of the band in the end. But it might not be too long. I adjudicated at the European Championship last year, where the band that came fourth was from Gothenburg in Sweden, and we were virtually tossing up as to whether to give them third place or not, which would have meant they had beaten Cory, who were

National Champions at the time. It's getting close. What they haven't got is beautiful cornet playing, but then neither have we these days. If they continue to improve, it won't be long before a surprise happens.

PATRICK HOWARTH: *Are there any other changes you would like to see in the wider field of banding?*

BRAM GAY: I should like to see bands more genuinely interested in the art of music. They are interested in the band, but not music, I think.

PATRICK HOWARTH: *Do you think the modern repertoire has helped promote musical appreciation?*

BRAM GAY: Yes, I do, but what really stops bands appreciating music with a capital 'M' is the lack of a classical background. When your father and I were kids, brass bands played opera selections all the time. When bands were at their peak in terms of popularity (in 1930 there were twelve thousand bands in this country, apart from the Salvation Army) they had audiences for park concerts or pier concerts because there was very little music about. If you wanted to hear Tchaikovsky you went to hear a band play it. Not orchestral Tchaikovsky, perhaps, but that public liked bands. I learnt a lot about music from playing Tchaikovsky for Fred Mortimer, and it was genuine Tchaikovsky, I can tell you. Whether he ever heard Tchaikovsky himself, God knows, but he certainly conducted it as if he had. It was better Tchaikovsky than a lot of Tchaikovsky I hear in the concert hall today, much better. There is a point in Tchaikovsky's Fourth Symphony that he used to make all the time which seems to me to be self-evidently correct, musically from the score, which I have never yet heard from any important conductor and which should be looked at, seriously.

Bands don't play arranged music any more. What are they looking for today? Mock-Stravinsky, the Lego-music written by the brass band specialists – I don't know. They haven't got an audience, so why not play a few tunes, a few Sullivan selections or Tchaikovsky arranged Rimmer? I believe, no, I know that your modern music enthusiast in the orchestra, the man who loves to play Henze, plays Henze against a background of Mozart – sitting firmly on that beautiful foundation, he can enjoy anything from Bach to Henze or Stockhausen. But if you haven't got that background, what have you got?

You ask me what changes I should like to see. I'm not that ambitious; I am just hoping for the survival of brass bands. I'm not looking forward to improvement or the development of banding, I'm just really hoping it's going to survive.

PATRICK HOWARTH: *Do you really think it's reached that drastic a stage?*

BRAM GAY: It's reaching the crunch very quickly, in my opinion. There may be a case for some of us getting together, sitting down and talking, to see what can be done.

PATRICK HOWARTH: *I should have thought widening contesting and other activities to include European bands must be one part of a solution.*

BRAM GAY: It must be good, and fortunately we are spreading abroad nicely, although in contemporary music. The Swedes invite me to

Gothenburg to play arranged Mozart because they have never played anything
written more than ten years back. They
thought Mozart would be fun and it was –
the Organ Fantasia arranged Sargent and
The Magic Flute Overture, or Elgar's
'Enigma' Variations. Tunes. The band had
never played anything like it. So I'm a kind
of antiques expert there, a sort of banding
Hogwood.

Unless some of us can find a solution as
to where the brass band is gooiing, then it
will not go anywhere. It has been chasing
its tail for a long time. It was chasing its tail
when we started the Granada Festival; one
year was like another, a cycleeee of winning or losing, on the same musical and
intellectual level all the time. Then we
made a slightly eccentric move, we slightly
bent the whole thing, which was mainly
down to your father and me and Arthur
Taylor, God bless him. Since then it has
been doing nothing; there's no new bent,
no new input. There is not as big a public
for the brass band now as there was then,
we have to face that. The BBC has
abandoned its *Best of Brass* competition,
which I thought was desperately bad anyway – I was glad to see it go because it was
so bad, but it was a pity because it was
exposure. They abandoned it because of
very clear scientific market research, dip-
ping into what the public wanted, and they
came up with the conclusion that nobody
wanted it. You may say that's because it's
a minority programme, but that's only
partially true. I can tell you that Granada
Television are carefully *not* doing the
market research on their one programme a
year, because if they did do it they know

what they would find – a complete no-no, and they'd take it off. But they feel a responsibility to 'Granadaland', as they call it, where many of the bands come from, to do something for the local culture; but every year they look at it again and ask themselves if they can really go on with it. Every year they fail to sell it to the other regions, until they blackmail them into taking it in the end, to be shown in the middle of the night.

So I would say that the brass band has lost its public already, and for the best possible reasons: the level of musical supply given by the brass band through its cultural history has been superseded by the media and communications. If you want light entertainment these days you don't go to the park, or, if you do, you put on a headset and listen to Mahler while walking the dog – you don't sit down and listen to a brass band play something arranged. You cannot fault the public's judgement in that way. There is no reason why the public should listen to something it doesn't want to hear. At the moment all the efforts of the best bands seem to be going into extraordinary scores, extraordinary experiments. John Fletcher[1] once said about tuba solos: 'Tuba concerti are written by tuba players for tuba players to play to tuba players.' Now the brass band is getting perilously near the Fletcher definition – brass band music is being written by bandsmen for bandsmen to play to bandsmen, *but the bandsmen don't listen, either!*

1 Tuba player with the London Symphony Orchestra and the Philip Jones Brass Ensemble.

Outside the top section what have you got? Seven hundred bands all practising for the next contest – two or three pieces a year and half a dozen little parks, concerts or fêtes with a captive audience; apart from that, they have no audience. I think that bands have got to be encouraged to make their audience. Some bands do already. I live near the Cambridge Co-op Band, where David Read conducts. You'd say nobody would be interested in bands in Cambridge, no one would give that band a concert, so they book a hall and work at getting an audience in, and now they can fill the Corn Exchange. It's not a typical brass band audience, but once you get them in you can build an audience. Other bands just sit on their bottoms all year round and wait for someone to ask them to play. No one asks them. Bands are in the same position as a young, emerging professional brass ensemble or string quartet. No one's going to offer them work. They have to make it. If you wish to be a string quartet, go out and book your church, do your own bill-posting, play your concert and see if anyone comes. Bands have reached that point, but they don't know it yet.

I really feel it's quite urgent, and I'm not the only one who feels so. In fact I don't know anyone who isn't worried by the situation, but I know few people who are doing anything about it. There is probably a need for a think-tank – an informal one, because the bands would never vote one in – to sit down quite soon and see what needs to be done. I suggested a few years back that we needed a Mortimer Society, for want of a better term – a group of twenty people doing the thinking, and influencing and bending and leaning on people. When I thought of it, it was just a nice idea, but it's fast becoming a desperate need.

4

Melodies

1900–1970

THE HISTORY OF brass bands during the first seventy years of this century has been dominated by dynamic personalities. Enderby Jackson, John Gladney, Edwin Swift and Alexander Owen, the most influential characters of the nineteenth century, all have their equivalents in the twentieth, but it was their combined inspiration which fired the enthusiasm of the man who was to lead the sometimes reluctant brass bands into the modern age.

It is interesting to note the effect that brass bands can have on the open-minded initiate – his life is not so much changed as completely taken over. What happened to Enderby Jackson at Burton Constable in 1845, happened to John Henry Iles at Belle Vue in 1898. A wealthy businessman and keen musician, Iles was in Manchester on a business trip in September 1898; looking for entertainment, he took the advice of a hotel porter and went to the brass band contest at Belle Vue. There he witnessed a victory by Wyke Temperance and Edwin Swift, with Hucknall Temperance and John Gladney as runners-up. Alexander Owen, who conducted ten bands that day, took third prize with Lea Mills and fifth with Kettering Rifles. Iles's reaction is best described in his own words: 'Inspired by what I had heard, I returned to London with a clear-cut vision at the back of my mind. I resolved to make the wonderful musical achievements of these northern pitmen, and other comparatively poor men, known to the whole world, and from these humble beginnings to widen the scope of the Brass Band Movement until its benefits could be enjoyed by other working-men musicians all over the country ...' It is also possible that, impressed by the size of the crowds, Iles saw money in brass bands.

57

Iles was not the sort of man to prevaricate once an idea was in his head, and the first thing he did to realize his dream was to buy the *British Bandsman* (whose previous owner, Samuel Cope, stayed on as editor) and the music publishers R. Smith and Co. Ltd. But Iles was above all an entrepreneur; his role-model was Enderby Jackson, and it was Jackson's Crystal Palace contests of the 1860s that Iles wanted to emulate. But, like Jackson, Iles had first to prove his organizational abilities and the drawing-power of brass bands to the Crystal Palace management.

These were the years of the Boer War, and the country was in the grip of patriotic fervour. Iles decided to tap this feeling by staging a Grand Patriotic Concert of brass bands at the Royal Albert Hall, featuring ten bands from all parts of the country playing both individually and as a vast massed band, 'the largest orchestra in the world', as Iles referred to it. Understanding the value of publicity, he joined forces with the *Daily Mail's* Kipling Fund, but his greatest coup was to recruit the reluctant Sir Arthur Sullivan to conduct the massed bands in his arrangement of Kipling's patriotic poem 'The Absent-Minded Beggar' – an arrangement to which Iles also owned the publishing rights. Despite a lukewarm reception from the London press, the concert was a success. Ten thousand tickets were sold and everyone was carried away by the emotion of the evening – even Sullivan, who asked of Iles: 'What can be done for these fellows?'

As luck would have it, Sullivan was one of the directors of the Crystal Palace, and with his support a National Brass Band Championship was organized for July 1900. Bands were invited from all over the country – the Belle Vue Championships had become an almost exclusively Yorkshire and Lancastrian affair – and the ever-important cheap rail excursions were provided for the bands and their followers. Iles decided that the contest should be graded in three sections, so that lesser bands could also compete in London and have the chance to hear the 'cracks' perform. Twenty-nine bands entered, twelve in the top section, including Besses and Black Dyke, who competed for the magnificent Thousand Guinea Trophy, originally presented at choral contests during the previous century. Despite a large and enthusiastic crowd, the event was not a runaway success. The northern bands especially were unconvinced, particularly by the results, which gave the trophy to unfancied Denton Original and Alex Owen. Indeed, it was many years before the northern establishment lost its mistrust of this London businessman, John Henry Iles – and, not surprisingly, some northern bands did not enter in 1901, reducing the number of entries to twenty-seven. However, Iles was nothing if not persevering; if he made mistakes, he learnt quickly from them. In 1902 he tried to introduce regional qualification contests, but local hostility forced him to abandon them: the 'cracks' did not see why they had to win the right to compete in London, the lesser bands did not fancy their chances of ever getting there if they had to beat the 'cracks' at home first. Iles seems to have backed down on this occasion, but he kept the idea of regionals at the back of his mind, believing them to be the only way to make his contest truly the 'National'. Other rules introduced in 1902 were more successful, especially in tightening up on band personnel at contests and on professionalism, a problem that was to dog banding for many years. The number of entries rose dramatically in 1902 – ninety bands competed, twenty-one in the top section. Entries continued to rise, until in 1910 200 bands applied but only 160 could be accepted, owing to lack of space and time. Clearly, the National Brass Band Championships were established – now Iles could introduce innovations.

Iles had new ideas for broadening the scope of brass bands both within and outside the world of contesting. His greatest service to the future of contests, and to the respectability and, therefore, the more widespread acceptance of banding, was his commissioning of original test-pieces. The test-piece had become the norm at Belle Vue and Iles had followed this example when founding his Crystal Palace championships. However, all test-pieces used at Belle Vue between 1872 and 1908 had been arrangements by Lieutenant Charles Godfrey, who always adjudicated as well, and there was growing dissatisfaction in some quarters at the quality and variety of the works chosen. Iles decided to provide a challenging alternative – in 1913 he commissioned a piece from the composer Percy Fletcher. The result was 'Labour and Love', a tone-poem, and rather a departure from the operatic selection everyone was accustomed to. Irwell Springs were judged the winners, and the test-piece was declared a success. For the 1914 competition Cyril Jenkins wrote 'Coriolanus', a symphonic poem based on Shakespeare's tragedy. Unfortunately its first performance was delayed by the outbreak of war – the military took over the Crystal Palace, halting the London contests – and it was not heard until 1920.

After the war Iles restarted the National Championships and began to commission more new works, the first being Cyril Jenkins's 'Life Divine', considered horrendously difficult at the time but soon to become a classic of the brass band repertoire. In the late 1920s and early 1930s Iles became even more ambitious when he persuaded four leading orchestral composers to write for band. Gustav Holst wrote his 'Moorside Suite' for the Crystal Palace finals of 1928; it was hoped he would write more, but he died six years later. The greatest coup was at the Championships of 1930, with Sir Edward Elgar's 'Severn Suite' as the test-piece. John Ireland wrote two National test-pieces, his 'Downland Suite' in 1932 and the 'Comedy Overture' in 1934. Last of the four was Arthur Bliss, whose suite 'Kenilworth' was the test-piece in 1935.

But Iles did not want to use only established composers; he wanted to promote new talent. In 1925 he offered a prize of one hundred guineas for the best new work for brass band. Denis Wright's overture 'Joan of Arc' won and was used as the Championship test-piece that year. Also in 1925 came the first original test-piece for Belle Vue, 'Macbeth' by Thomas Keighley. This was commissioned by Iles, too, because he had led a consortium which had bought the Manchester pleasure gardens earlier in the year. The dissatisfaction at the Belle Vue Championships had continued – in 1923 four of the leading bands, Black Dyke, Foden's, Harton and St Hilda Colliery, had not even entered. If anything, it had increased when the London contest had begun to set the bands challenging original pieces. However, the new management and new test-pieces soon reawakened enthusiasm.

Iles's commissions were undoubtedly popular with the bands, and helped to improve standards of technique and musicianship. Indeed, so quickly did bands of all grades progress that Percy Fletcher's 'Labour and Love', the National test-piece of 1913 that was regarded as so hard to play and so difficult to understand when first performed, was used as the test-piece for the lower-grade bands' contest at Belle Vue in July 1926.

Under Iles's guidance both the National and the Belle Vue contests continued to develop. So popular were the Crystal Palace championships that by 1920 there were six sections, including one for reed band, another for boys' band, a Junior Cup and a Junior Shield. In 1922 Iles dropped the reed band section but added a sixth brass section, making the National an all-brass occasion. In the same year bands were made to perform in concert formation, sitting down facing their conductor, rather than standing up in the traditional square formation. It would be some time before other contests, including Belle Vue, followed suit. However, Belle Vue had introduced a new contest series in 1922 to complement the July and September events; this series was for lower-section bands and was held in May. Iles, who had bought Belle Vue in 1925, restructured these contests in 1931 into the May Brass Band Festival, adding a marching band section. A band could start in the bottom section at the May Festival and work its way up to the July contest, which was now divided into two classes, and from there progress to the September championships. Not all of Iles's innovations caught on, however; his Deportment and Marching contest, based on Australian Quickstep contests, was cancelled soon after the Second World War. On the other hand, the introduction of massed band concerts at Belle Vue was as successful as it had been in London – at least, the audiences loved them, as did Iles who conducted; the bandsmen themselves were less keen because, by all accounts, Iles was a dreadful conductor.

Iles also had great influence on brass banding away from the contest stage, for he was one of the first to organize brass band tours. Besses o' th' Barn and Alexander Owen were the lucky combination Iles chose to promote after their victory at the Crystal Palace in 1903. The following year Iles sent them on an extensive British tour. In 1905 they again toured the country, giving a performance for the royal family at Windsor Castle. Most significantly, they also travelled to France, with the official blessing of Prime Minister Balfour, to help cement the entente cordiale. Besses played nearly two hundred concerts in 1905, but it was soon apparent that this had been just a warm-up.

Iles always thought on the large scale and his next project was a world tour, visiting America, Australia, New Zealand, Fiji, Hawaii and Canada, an ambitious enough programme today but, in the years before air travel, quite extraordinary. The tour lasted seventeen months, from July 1906 to December 1907, and everywhere Besses went they received a rapturous welcome from British emigrants and the local people, many of whom had probably never heard a brass band before. But Iles had not yet exhausted his plans, and in 1909 Besses set off on another massive expedition, which this time included a visit to South Africa. There can be no doubting that these tours, while exhausting for those involved, played an important part in spreading brass banding throughout the world and helping to make it the cosmopolitan musical force it is today.

Iles gave fifty years of his life to bands, but after the Second World War he was spent, both physically and financially, since some of his speculations outside banding had gone badly. The National Championships had stopped during the war, as they had done in the first war. After the destruction of the Crystal Palace by fire in 1936, the last two pre-war contests had been held on a trial basis at Alexandra Palace in North London, but that cavernous building had proved to be unpopular with bandsmen and audiences alike. So the National needed a new home and financial backing. The *Daily Herald* had been impressed with the size of the crowd of 20,000 which had attended the 1944 Belle Vue Championships, and agreed to support Iles's reorganized contest, to be held at the Royal Albert Hall in September. Eight regional contests were arranged, despite hostility in

Yorkshire and Lancashire, with each area sending two bands
to London; only the defending champions were automatical-
ly invited. Seventeen bands took part in a tremendously
successful Championship finals in 1945, performing another
new commission, Denis Wright's 'Overture for an Epic
Occasion'. There was one problem, however: the Albert
Hall was too small to accommodate everyone who wanted
tickets – a problem that continues to this day. The lower
sections were unable to find a London venue at all in 1945,
so their finals were moved to Belle Vue and staged the week
before the Championship section event. The Belle Vue
contests themselves had continued throughout the war years
and, after slight pruning back, they carried on as before.
When Iles died, in May 1951, both contests were firmly
established and running smoothly, which knowledge must
have given great comfort at the end to this remarkable man.

Who could possibly replace John Henry Iles? The answer
was, of course, nobody; rather, the two contests were run by
different teams. At Belle Vue Iles's son, H. F. B. Iles, took
over as manager, with Frank Parker as contest organizer, a
job he had already done brilliantly for 24 years. The London
contest, on the other hand, was under the control of the
Daily Herald and its organizing secretary, E. Vaughan
Morris.

The National turned out to be the more troublesome of
the two, primarily owing to problems of space and the
economic fragility of its sponsors. Fortunately, in Vaughan
Morris the bands had found another human dynamo who
was equal to any challenge. In the early 1950s the London
event was running well – the originally unpopular area
qualifying contests had become established and were gradually handed over to area committees who organized them
under the banner of the *Daily Herald*. In 1952 the National
Brass Band Contesting Council was set up, consisting of area
representatives and Vaughan Morris. This council aimed to
co-ordinate the London contests, in particular giving fair
representation to each region; later in the year organizers of
other contests, including Belle Vue, joined, making it a
more comprehensive body. Vaughan Morris continued the
commissioning of original test-pieces, and the late 1950s and

1960s saw the rise to prominence of the composers Eric Ball and Gilbert Vinter. But the council's biggest headache was still the demand for tickets, which simply could not be satisfied by the Royal Albert Hall. In 1952 and 1953 the Empress Hall at Earls Court was tried; but in 1954, when the three lower sections returned to London from their exile at Belle Vue, the Metropolitan Police, worried about the influx of so many people into the area for the big day, suggested that the Championship section be moved back to the Albert Hall and the lower-section contests staged at other venues around Kensington. To help ease the ticket situation, festival concerts of massed bands were introduced on the evening after the contest and also on the following night, so that at least three times as many people had a chance of seeing something.

No sooner had one problem been partially solved than a new one appeared, this time at the *Daily Herald* itself. The paper had undoubtedly been influenced in its decision to sponsor the championships by the size of the potential new readership that so popular a movement represented, and to this end a weekly column had been devoted to band news and features. But this was a time of social change and the new readership never appeared – although, even if if had, it could not on its own have solved the *Herald's* financial problems. The paper ceased publication in 1964, but fortunately the championships were handed over to a sister publication, *The People;* Vaughan Morris went with them as promoter. The contests were trimmed down, however. The regional qualifiers were abandoned, the National Brass Band Contesting Council was scrapped, and the National became an invitation-only event. Ironically, the regionals were an accepted part of the championships by now, so some areas carried on organizing their own pre-London heats, with Yorkshire the first to do so.

The People did not remain associated with brass bands for very long, and in 1966 handed over complete responsibility for the National Festival to Vaughan Morris. Now in sole charge, Vaughan Morris decided to introduce a World Championship. As banding was becoming ever more popular abroad, an international competition was becoming more of a possibility. Therefore, in 1969, Vaughan Morris invited a Dutch band to compete at the National and, rather dubiously, renamed it the World Championship. The next year he reorganized the contest yet again. On this occasion six British bands were invited to compete in the World Championship section, with a solitary European band, the Concorde Band from Copenhagen, representing the rest of the world. The National continued as before, with bands winning their invitations in regional qualifying heats, and the eventual winners gaining automatic entry to the Championship of the World. This was not a very satisfactory arrangement, however, because the world title could not really be taken seriously and the National had been somewhat debased by losing six of the top bands from the field of competitors. Not surprisingly, the World Championship was dropped after 1971, the year of Vaughan Morris's retirement, and the National soon got back into its stride once again. Belle Vue was in the capable hands of Harry Mortimer by this time and running smoothly, much less beset by trouble than its sister contest. The two great annual battles of brass were intact and secure, ready to face the onslaught of new ideas and new music in the 1970s.

If John Henry Iles and E. Vaughan Morris had been the 'Enderby Jacksons' of the twentieth century, who had replaced Gladney, Swift and Owen as the dominant musical personalities? Owen remained active until his death in 1920, but much of his energy had been spent trekking round the world with Besses o' th' Barn, rather than on the contest platform. Edwin Swift died in 1904, much mourned by the many bands he had trained. In the same year Gladney won his last major title, at Belle Vue with Black Dyke, and in 1906 this combination toured America, beating arch-rivals Besses across the Atlantic by a couple of months. With the three great men absent, a new man stepped into the limelight, the 'king' of brass bands, William Rimmer.

Rimmer was from Southport, born into a musical family – his father was bandmaster of the 3rd Volunteer Brigade, King's Liverpool Regiment. William had begun his career playing the cornet in the Southport Rifle Band before becoming a top soloist with bands such as Besses and

Kingston Mills. Towards the end of the last century he began training two bands, Wingates Temperance and Irwell Springs, both relatively unknown; but, more importantly, he became the music editor of F. Richardson's *Cornet Brass and Military Band Journal* and earned himself a reputation as a top-class arranger and composer, especially of marches. When Rimmer at last arrived on the contest platform, he made a tremendous impact. Between 1905 and 1909 he had consecutive victories at both the Crystal Palace and Belle Vue, including two doubles with Wingates Temperance in 1906 and 1907, one double with Irwell Springs in 1905, and the first success for Foden's Motor Works Band, a double in 1909. Then suddenly, at the height of his powers, he retired from contesting to conduct the Southport Municipal Military Band, a crack professional outfit. He did not completely abandon brass bands, however, since he continued to write and arrange for the medium; his musical legacy, at his death in 1936, was almost without rival in the affections of bandsmen.

Rimmer's immediate successor as top band trainer and conductor was William Halliwell, who had an unbroken string of victories in London and at Belle Vue over the next four years. The talented Halliwell, who came from Roby Mill, near Wigan, had been a church organist at sixteen, a cornet soloist at seventeen, and bandmaster of Upholland Temperance at the age of twenty. Two years later, in 1887, he went to Wigan Rifle Band as solo cornet, returning in 1893 as conductor, after various musical activities which included some orchestral work. By the time he began his remarkable series of victories, therefore, he was widely experienced and knowledgeable. Like Rimmer before him, William Halliwell conducted all the best bands of his day – between 1910 and 1936 he won at Belle Vue and London on an incredible twenty-seven occasions (eight with Foden's Motor Works, four with both Brighouse and Rastrick and St Hilda Colliery, three with Wingates Temperance, two with Black Dyke Mills, and one with Munn and Felton's, Besses o' th' Barn, Luton Red Cross, Irwell Springs, Hebden Bridge, and Perfection Soap Works).

During this extraordinary period only two men came even

close to challenging Halliwell's supremacy. The first was J. A. Greenwood, a protégé of Rimmer's, who had been persuaded by his mentor to play professionally with the New Brighton Tower Band. After the collapse of this ensemble Greenwood began training a number of lower-section bands, among them a struggling band from South Shields, St Hilda Colliery. He took this band from the Junior Cup section of the National to the Championship section in just four years (1906–9), but was replaced by Halliwell when the band won in London in 1912. He was compensated for his disappointment two years later, when he and Black Dyke were victorious at Belle Vue in 1914. Other Belle Vue successes followed, with Horwich Railway Mechanics' Institute Band, a completely new outfit, and with Creswell Colliery Band; Greenwood also twice took the National title, with Horwich RMI in 1922 and Marsden Colliery in 1925.

If J. A. Greenwood provided the main opposition to William Halliwell during the years of the Great War and the 1920s, Fred Mortimer and his Foden's Motor Works Band filled the role during the early 1930s.

Fred Mortimer's father had been a member of the famous Wyke Temperance Band, so it was not surprising that Fred learnt the cornet. At the age of twenty-one he was appointed bandmaster to his local band, Hebden Bridge; his job was to prepare the band for their professional conductor, who would add the finishing touches before a contest. Under the professional guidance of William Rimmer and William Halliwell, successive conductors at Hebden Bridge, Fred Mortimer became the finest band trainer in the country. Halliwell in particular was to play an important part in the lives of the Mortimer family, his first contribution being Fred's appointment as band trainer at another of Halliwell's bands, a relatively unknown southern outfit, Luton Red Cross.

The Mortimers moved south in 1910, and the following year Hebden Bridge Band, the first to benefit from the Mortimer treatment, won at Belle Vue. Fred's efforts to achieve similar results in Luton, however, were cut short by the outbreak of war – though Luton did appear at the

Crystal Palace Championships in 1913, including in their line-up Fred's eldest son, cleven-year-old Harry. After the war the Luton Band was rebuilt, with both Harry and his younger brother Alex among the players, and an all-out attack on the National was prepared. In 1920 Luton were placed fourth. They slipped to sixth place the next year, but were runners-up at the following year's contest. In 1923, with their performance of 'Oliver Cromwell' by Henry Geehl, they became the only southern band ever to win either of the two major championships. Suitably impressed, Halliwell asked Alex, a brilliant euphonium player, to join his top band, Foden's Motor Works. This turned out to be a preliminary move, for a year later the whole family returned to the North: Fred had been appointed bandmaster of Foden's.

Foden's had been successful before the Mortimers' arrival – their victories included the Belle Vue title five times between 1909 and 1915, and the National title in 1910, all but one of these conducted by Halliwell – but under Fred Mortimer's leadership they became indisputably the top band of the years between the wars. Their record speaks for itself. Under Halliwell's baton the band won a hat-trick of victories at Belle Vue between 1926 and 1928. In 1929 Halliwell handed over the baton to Fred, conceding that the band played better for their bandmaster than for their professional conductor. Under Fred, Foden's won in London in 1930 and followed this with another two hat-tricks in 1932–4 and 1936–8; as hat-trick winners they were barred from competing in 1935. Unfortunately Fred refused to enter them at Belle Vue, because he felt that the noise of the funfair outside the King's Hall obtruded on the music within. The London contests were suspended during the Second World War, and the great combination never won again. However, the band was to taste victory in the National of 1950, on this occasion conducted by Harry Mortimer.

Harry Mortimer is the most famous bandsman of all; his is the name most people associate with brass bands. His extraordinary career is without parallel, for not only has he taken on the mantle of the great musicians like Owen,

Rimmer and Halliwell, and the master administrators like
Jackson and Iles, but he has also looked ahead to the
promotion of new ideas and music.

Harry started cornet lessons with his father at the age of
five, made his National début at eleven, conducted the
Luton Junior Band when he was fourteen, and was a teenage
professional in a theatre pit orchestra during the First World
War. By the time he arrived at Foden's in 1924, aged
twenty-two, he was already a veteran. While solo cornet at
Foden's, he also started a busy professional career on the
provincial concert circuit, in demand as a soloist in popular
works such as Handel's *Messiah*. He soon graduated to the
northern orchestras as a trumpet player, joining the Hallé as
third trumpet in 1927. By 1930 he was principal trumpet with
the Liverpool Philharmonic, returning to the Hallé a year
later to fill the same position. In 1935 he again left the
Hallé, to join the newly founded BBC Northern Orchestra,
where he played, among others, under Sir Thomas
Beecham. While pursuing his orchestral career, Harry still
found the time to play solo cornet in all of Foden's National
Championship triumphs and to become professional conductor to some small local bands, such as Congleton.

As conductor, Harry's name is most commonly associated
with the Fairey Aviation Works Band, which had been
started in 1937 by Sir Richard Fairey at his light aircraft
engineering works in Stockport. Just as Fred Mortimer and
Foden's had been the top combination of the 1930s, so
Harry Mortimer and Fairey's dominated the 1940s. Band
and conductor won at Belle Vue seven times between 1941
and 1950, and again in 1956; victories were recorded in
London in 1945, 1952 and 1954. Like other premier
conductors before him, Harry did not limit his activities to
one band, and he also tasted success with Bickershaw
Colliery Band in the 1946 Belle Vue Open, and won the
National Championships with Black Dyke Mills (1947, 1948
and 1949), Foden's (1950 and 1953) and Munn and Felton's
(1955).

As if such statistics were not enough, there is still one
aspect of Harry's banding life that we have not yet touched
upon. When he retired from contest conducting in 1956, the

main reason was pressure of work in his other job as Supervisor of Brass and Military Bands at BBC Radio. Band broadcasts had begun in the 1920s: the earliest is thought to have been given in April 1923 by Clydebank Burgh Band from Scotland. These broadcasts had made a whole new audience aware of brass bands – by the 1930s nine million radio licences had been issued – although there were only five programmes a week which featured bands. When Harry joined the BBC in 1942 he embarked upon a twenty-two year campaign of battling for more air-time and defending that air-time once it had been won. The number of band programmes rose to an average of sixteen a week, many of them live broadcasts, and featuring military and Salvation Army bands as well as brass bands. Sadly, after Harry's departure from radio the amount of available air-time has diminished again – indeed, in the very week in which Radio 2 broadcast a three-part series to commemorate Harry Mortimer's eighty-fifth birthday (in April 1987), there were only two bands featured on BBC Radio, and both of them were service bands.

Through his orchestral experience Harry also led the way in encouraging interest in bands among orchestral conductors. Sir Hamilton Harty of the Hallé Orchestra had advised Foden's on their preparation of Elgar's 'Severn Suite' in 1930. Sir Adrian Boult, Sir Malcolm Sargent and Sir John Barbirolli had conducted massed band concerts at Belle Vue during the war which were promoted and recorded by the BBC under the direction of Harry and Dr Denis Wright. At their suggestion such concerts were introduced on the evening after the National Championships, and the Festival Concerts have become an important part of the event, with eminent orchestral conductors often presiding.

Harry Mortimer is the last truly dominant figure in the mould of Gladney, Rimmer or Halliwell. These days conductors may conduct more than one band, but no one man has all the top bands under his baton. Few have come close to matching Harry's contest record and none has come close to matching his continuing contribution.

The problem of professionalism has troubled brass banding virtually since its beginnings in the early nineteenth century, and to some extent continues to do so today. One of the bandsman's proudest boasts is that he is an amateur musician; contesting bands in particular must be amateur, with only the conductor allowed to derive his principal income from music.

During the latter part of the nineteenth century new regulations were introduced to try to prevent 'professionals' competing: it was said at this time that the players in the leading bands were so well known that any professional whose face didn't fit would be spotted instantly. Nevertheless, the rules were bent – Alexander Owen was hired by Meltham Mills Band in the 1870s to play the cornet, and there was no question of his working in the mill itself (in fact, he did not even live anywhere near the mill, but ran a public house at Stalybridge, on the opposite side of the Pennines). After the turn of the century John Henry Iles tried to tighten the rules of his new London contests, and similar attempts were made at Belle Vue. These were successful to some extent, since they managed to limit a player's professionalism to a single band; it was a step towards curbing the use of 'borrowed men', a system whereby bands could hire top soloists for the day of a contest in order to lend the band that extra title-winning sparkle. However, the star soloists were still playing, albeit with one regular band.

The entire issue came to a head in 1926, when the St Hilda Colliery Band won at the Crystal Palace for the fifth time. Industrial disputes had closed the colliery itself in 1925 and, rather than starve, the band had gone on the road, although some members, probably foreseeing trouble, had left to join other outfits. As St Hilda's was one of the top bands in the country, a number of well-paid dates were soon set up – so many, in fact, that the band's coach, which had originally cost 2,000 guineas, was paid for in saved travelling expenses alone in a little over a year. They also continued to compete. Some conductors at the 1926 National complained that St Hilda's had become a professional band, and Iles upheld their objections. In 1927, therefore, St Hilda's became the only brass band to go openly professional, and for ten years they were a popular attraction at the seaside, in parks, and on the theatre and concert circuit. But gradually the amount of work dwindled because, once the band had stopped contesting, they were less in the public eye and therefore less in demand, until they finally disbanded in September 1937.

St Hilda's may have accepted their fate gracefully, but there was still a problem with professionalism, for the moves against 'borrowed players' had ultimately proved unsuccessful. In 1928 Harry Mortimer wrote an open letter to the *British Bandsman* announcing his retirement as a 'borrowed man' because 'Friendship and goodwill of fellow bandsmen mean more to me than the £.s.d. of being borrowed', but it is not known whether anyone else followed suit. Innumerable ploys have been tried over the years to discourage the practice – players were made to sign in before appearing on stage at Belle Vue from 1930 onwards – but yet another warning about 'borrowed players' had to be issued in 1948. Even a National Registry of Brass Bandsmen, started after the war by the *Daily Herald,* has not been totally successful in cleaning up contesting.

The beginning of the twentieth century saw brass bands at the height of their popularity. These were the days when choirs and bands were the principal areas of working-class cultural activity, and the main access to music for a working-class audience was through these two areas. The first half of the century, however, also saw the beginnings of a massive social upheaval which has diminished this audience and even destroyed some bands in the process.

'The war to end all wars', the First World War, was the catalyst in much of the change: many had said that, after it, nothing would ever be the same again, and this was to be true of banding. Bandsmen had joined up as enthusiastically as the rest of the population, a band often volunteering en masse for musical duties – Fred Mortimer and seven members of the Luton Red Cross Band were drafted into the 36th Division of the Royal Irish Rifles as bandsmen, but spent the early part of the war as stretcher bearers (presumably someone thought that members of a 'Red Cross' band must be first-aid experts, although nobody knew why the band bore that title). Those who remained at home tried to keep their bands together, with young players joining the veterans. Although the National Championships at the Crystal Palace had to stop, Belle Vue continued to hold contests throughout the war, providing some sense of continuity; quartet and solo competitions were also organized to keep the spirit of contesting alive.

It is difficult to be sure exactly what effect the war had on banding – of the one million soldiers from the British Army who were killed, 750,000 were from the United Kingdom itself, and some of those were certainly bandsmen; a far greater number were injured. The major bands seem to have recovered fairly quickly, but smaller bands must have had a much harder time of it.

Already shaken by the war, banding, like so much else, continued to suffer during peacetime. In many respects the Depression of the 1920s and 1930s was more disastrous than the war. In 1920 twenty-five colliery bands were forced to pull out of the National because of a miners' strike – ironically, the contest was won by St Hilda Colliery, who were presumably unaffected by the industrial action. Proposals to cut wages and increase working hours at pits eventually led to the General Strike of 1926, and by the beginning of the 1930s unemployment had risen to three million for the first time ever. Under these conditions bands reacted in a variety of ways. Foden's, the most successful band of the 1930s, owed some of their success to a fairly stable line-up – all the musicians had jobs in the factory, supplementing their income through concert fees. As men were laid off or put on short-time, Foden's bandsmen clung on to the band as the only means of earning any money at all. As we have seen, St Hilda's, whose colliery had closed in 1925, had become semi-professional and, from 1927, a full-time professional outfit. It is surprising that they lasted even ten years on the concert circuit during a period of such adverse economic conditions. Other bands were weakened or destroyed when their members either tried to turn professional or moved south to look for work, incidentally giving southern banding a much-needed boost. Works bands suffered more than subscription bands on the whole. A subscription band, going into a decline, could still survive while it looked for new members and waited for the situation to improve, because the band generally owned its instruments and music, but if a struggling industrialist decided to axe his works' band, that was that: music and instruments were sold to help balance the books, and a great band like Hebburn Colliery, National Champions in 1904, disappeared overnight.

The Depression had done so much damage that the impact of the Second World War was not as cataclysmic as it might otherwise have been. The survival techniques learnt during the Great War were put into practice. Quartet and solo competitions were organized and concerts arranged at army camps. While all those of military age joined up, some bands were kept going with a mixture of youth and experience; others were put on ice until the hostilities were over. The National Championships were stopped once again, but Belle Vue continued, with new contests for Air Training Corps Bands, Fire Service Bands, Home Guard and ARP Bands (some of which were established groups in new guise), as well as the traditional events. Some bandsmen were in reserved occupations, which allowed their bands to stay together – in particular the Fairey Aviation Works Band, the most successful band of the 1940s. One positive effect of the war was the introduction of women musicians into the bands to replace the absent men; a few even managed to retain their places after 1945, which sowed the seeds of greater female involvement in banding. In general, not as many bands disappeared during the second war as during the first, and indeed peacetime was again to bring more problems than the war years themselves.

In the late 1940s and early 1950s bands began to try to recover and rebuild, but there were many obstacles to be negotiated. For some, nationalization of the coal-mines was the greatest. Certain colliery owners had cultivated their bands, often giving the bandsmen safe surface-work which allowed them as much free time to rehearse as possible. Nationalization not only changed the management system, it changed the management itself. What was good for the industry was not necessarily good for the bands, for some of the new pit managers were not band enthusiasts and at their collieries the bands often went into decline. The most tragic case was the loss of Bickershaw Colliery Band, Belle Vue Champions in 1940, 1943 and 1946. In 1947 their patron, the brass band fanatic Lieutenant-Colonel Hart, realizing that he was going to lose his pits, offered to support the band privately after nationalization. The band rested for a month during October while the Colonel made his arrangements, but, depressed and unable to adjust to the post-war world, Hart killed himself, and indirectly his beloved band.

Subscription bands may not have disappeared at the same rate as works bands, but many found it very difficult to re-establish themselves at the top. Even a band with a history like Besses o' th' Barn had hit hard times – by 1952 the band had only one engagement in its diary; it would not be until the late 1950s that it would re-emerge as a force to be reckoned with. Only Brighouse and Rastrick, the most successful subscription band of the war and post-war period, was able to pose a serious threat to the surviving works bands.

Despite all the gloom and despondency, there was also some good news, for post-war industrial expansion brought with it a crop of new works bands. H. B. Hawley, managing director of Hammond's Sauce Works, formed, trained and conducted a new band himself, and within a decade they were finalists at the National. The Co-operative Wholesale Society in Manchester formed a band which, with their conductor Eric Ball, became Belle Vue Open Champions within a few years of their foundation. This boom in the numbers of works bands continued into the 1950s, until social and economic conditions caused the bubble to burst, and some bands vanished almost as quickly as they had appeared.

Probably the greatest challenge to brass banding since the Second World War has been these social changes, particularly in people's leisure habits and social attitudes. The growth of radio certainly brought brass band music to a wider audience, but it also brought classical music, jazz, pop, and other diverse styles. As television grew in popularity in the mid-1950s, many people began to stay at home for their entertainment, and the new medium and brass bands have never enjoyed a prosperous relationship. There was suddenly a much greater choice of things to do, and if you wanted to listen to music you no longer had to rely on brass bands for access to the classics or the latest popular favourites; records and radio provided all forms of music in the original at the flick of a switch. In the 1960s Britain became the place where everything was new, and in comparison brass bands seemed terribly old-fashioned. New ideas such as a World Championship had been tried, but without any real success: clearly, if bands were to survive and progress in the 1970s, they needed a new image, new ideas and new music.

5

Xylophone Solo

An Administrator:
Ken Hirst

KEN HIRST spent his entire working life with the National
Coal Board, at various pits in the South Yorkshire Coalfield.
For over thirty years he has been Secretary of Grimethorpe
Colliery Band, one of the top contest and concert bands of
the post-war years. During this time the band has appeared
at the Henry Wood Promenade Concerts, on the South
Bank in London, and at a number of music festivals, all
venues not traditionally associated with brass bands. Ken
Hirst has also supervised tours of North America, Australia
and Europe. He lives in Grimethorpe, where Patrick
Howarth talked to him in November 1986.

PATRICK HOWARTH: *Did you come from a brass band background?*

KEN HIRST   No, not at all. In fact, all through my
childhood I didn't really know any brass
band players at all.

PATRICK HOWARTH: *Where were you born and brought up?*

KEN HIRST: I was born in a village called Goldthorpe, but we only stayed there about six
months. It's only about ten miles away
from here, actually.

PATRICK HOWARTH: *So you've always lived in this area?*

KEN HIRST: Oh, yes. From Goldthorpe we went to
Monk Breton and then Cudworth, where I
spent most of my young life. I only moved
to Grimethorpe when I got married, because my first job was at Grimethorpe
Colliery.

PATRICK HOWARTH: *Although you had always lived in this area, had you never been aware of the Grimethorpe Band?*

KEN HIRST: No. Even after I started work at Grimethorpe Colliery in 1943, for the first four or five years I was not particularly aware that there was a band here. I must have known George Thompson[1] and some of the players – I can remember seeing Jimmy Scott[2] wandering around the yard in his overalls. But it was not until some years later, when I was working in the manager's office at the pit, that I really began to be aware of it. There was a man called George Hespe who lived in Sheffield, and was quite well known in the band world; he was an ex-military band-master and came to Grimethorpe in 1947, I think. I vaguely remember that there was a 'stint strike' at Grimethorpe which lasted for about seven weeks, and they put George Hespe to work in the office with me – I mustn't misuse the word 'work', because I never remember him doing any! About six months later he left and was replaced by Harry Mileman, who did in fact do a good job of work. At this time the band secretary was a man called Reg Alderson, who had been secretary for a number of years. He became ill for three or four months, and Harry Mileman was virtually acting secretary. I helped Harry out by doing a lot of his correspondence in the office, which must have been the first time I found out much about the band.

1 Former conductor of Grimethorpe Colliery Band
2 James Scott, then a cornet player, is now conductor of Yorkshire Imperial Metals Band.

PATRICK HOWARTH: *Had you ever had any musical experience or background?*

KEN HIRST: The only musical education I had was learning the piano, from about the age of fourteen. I was never any great shakes as a piano player – in fact, I think Fred Partlett[1] would tell you I'm awful! But I could always play to amuse myself, although I was nowhere near being a performer. I can't really say that I've ever had an ear for music, but I do like good music, I like to hear it played well. I don't think I could have been secretary to a third- or fourth-rate brass band; it would have to be one of the best for me to be able to tolerate it.

PATRICK HOWARTH: *What was your job at the colliery when you started working there?*

KEN HIRST: I suppose they called it 'manager's clerk'. In those days there weren't many women around the place, there weren't any secretaries at the colliery, so I suppose I was the colliery manager's secretary. I looked after all his demands – attending meetings, taking minutes and so on. I remember I was getting thirty shillings a week in 1943. I asked the secretary of the colliery company, which was Carlton Main Colliery Co., for an increase in wages, because I was getting ten shillings a week less than the errand lad. They gave me exactly ten shillings a week extra, bringing me up to the magnificent sum of two pounds a week.

PATRICK HOWARTH: *So it was by chance, really, that you became involved with the band?*

---

1 Former cornet player with Grimethorpe

KEN HIRST:

Yes, I suppose it was. The people in the band got to know who I was, through working with Harry Mileman and others, like Bob Davidson, who still does a job of work for the band, Joe Armstrong[1] and Reg Alderson, the band secretary. When Reg decided to retire, some of the players approached me and asked me if I was interested in becoming secretary of the band. I didn't know that much about it, but, having worked with Harry Mileman a few years earlier, I knew a little about band affairs. At that time the position paid the princely sum of a pound a week – £50 a year – and for the early 1950s it was quite a good sum on top of my weekly wage; you might even say that initially I took the job on because it paid well. I might mention that today I get three times that amount, so if I get £150 compared with £50 then – well, there's no comparison, is there?

I agreed to become secretary at a meeting, where I answered all the questions as best I could. I'll always remember the solo trombone player questioning the fact that I might not be able to read music. I couldn't see what that had to do with being secretary of the band, and he was a bit flabbergasted when he found out that I *could* read music. I think he also suggested that the salary be cut to £25 a year initially because I was so raw, but he was overruled on that one.

PATRICK HOWARTH:

Did everyone in the band vote for whom they wanted as secretary?

KEN HIRST:

I think they must have done. It had always been agreed in Grimethorpe Col-

---

1 Former euphonium player

Barton Hall Works Band.

Author (back row, first left), Stan Howarth (brother — centre row, fourth from left), Oliver Howarth (father — front row centre, holding baton)

Barton Hall Works Band summer park concert —
conductor Oliver Howarth, vocalist Victor Galvin

Cannock Salvation Army Band

Black Dyke Mills Band in 1984   *Ron Massey*

Brighouse and Rastrick Band at Saddleworth   *Dennis Hussey*

· 1921–22 ·

· 1920 ·

· 1920–21 ·

· 1923 ·

· 1923–24 ·

WON OUTRIGHT

Black Dyke Mills Band in the 1920s

liery Band that the secretary was never a player. More often than not, the secretaries of other bands are themselves players. I've always thought that it's a great advantage for me not to be a player, because it means I can talk to people like our musical director and the professionals who come here in a way I couldn't if I was a player. There are times, of course, when I feel out of it, as if I don't belong to the organization because I am not a player. At times when they are performing, and giving a good performance, I think I'd like to be among them, but at the same time I know that in my position it's better that I'm not.

PATRICK HOWARTH: *What is your earliest memory as band secretary?*

KEN HIRST: The first competition I went to with the band, on the first Sunday in March 1953, was the local Sheffield CISWO[1] Brass Band Contest. I've been there every year since, making it thirty-four years of contests, which is a long time.

PATRICK HOWARTH: *What sort of a band was Grimethorpe in those days?*

KEN HIRST: Going back a few years from the early 1950s, when I got involved, Grimethorpe had been in the top flight until the end of the war, but then there had been a bit of a decline. A colliery not too far away decided to form a band; I don't think they had had one before, and they were offering higher wages and better jobs than at Grimethorpe, so quite a few players left to join this new colliery band, which was called Woolley (where Arthur Scargill

1 Coal Industries Social Welfare Organization

comes from). For about four or five years Grimethorpe went down as a playing combination until they had a bit of a recruitment drive in the early 1950s, when they got players coming down from Scotland, from Wales, and even one or two from the South. So when I took over as secretary in 1953, and started to go to all the competitions, we had quite a good combination, but we didn't score very often. Something was wrong somewhere. We had one or two changes of conductor; Harry Mileman came back again, then Andrew Owenson. By the end of the 1950s we'd decided that what we needed was a better conductor, and that basically we should go all out to get George Thompson back. George had been with the band during the war years and had quite a good reputation as a conductor; after spells with one or two bands he had ended up in Cornwall, which is a bit the backwoods of brass banding, really. He was interested in coming back to a band like Grimethorpe, and once we'd fixed him up with a job and a house, he came back full-time in 1959, although he took us to one to two contests before that. I think you could say that from 1959 onwards Grimethorpe Colliery Band has gone up and up and up.

The first time that we really scored was at Belle Vue in 1960, when we were placed third, and we've never really looked back from then on. We won the Open Championship of Great Britain in 1967 and 1969, and were placed third in the year in between. We are on the roll of honour of the National Championship as having won it in 1970, but I always say that we won the second section, because the World Championship was being held and some of the best bands were involved in that and not in the National Championship. For those people who remember, it never really happened; but we did win and it allowed us to be in the World Championship the next year, although that didn't do us much good either.

PATRICK HOWARTH: *What exactly is your job in the day-to-day running of the band?*

KEN HIRST: I suppose it should be an easy thing to explain, but when someone asks me that question I always get a little puzzled. Basically, the secretary of an organization like a brass band should be responsible for everything to do with administration; or you could put it another way by saying he's in charge of everything that's not to do with the musical side, which probably sums it up better than anything. He's supposed to deal with all correspondence, of course. I've a great reputation for not replying to any letters, by the way – you'll get Harry Mortimer saying 'I've received a letter from Ken Hirst and I've framed it!' What they say isn't strictly true; I do reply to a lot of letters, and I do write a lot of letters. So I deal with all correspondence involved with the band and the committee.

PATRICK HOWARTH: *How does the committee work?*

KEN HIRST: We supposedly have an election every year, when we put down a list of the names of all the band members, and we ask each member to put a mark by the six names he wants as committee members. On top of those six there's myself, and we usually ask the musical director to sit on the committee as a kind of ex-officio member, so that we can talk about questions relating to the musical side. We have no set pattern to our meetings. We basically agree that we ought to have a main meeting at least once every month; but we find that we've always got something to talk about on a day-to-day basis, and so we often end up having a meeting after every rehearsal, which becomes a bit of a bind in the end.

PATRICK HOWARTH: *What does the committee do?*

KEN HIRST: We are supposed to sit down, go through the correspondence, and then make decisions based on that. The only fly in the ointment is that if a meeting lasts two or three hours there's a lot of discussion in that amount of time, and only one person has any work to do afterwards: the poor old secretary. It's easy for someone to say 'I propose we do this' or 'I propose we do that', when there's only one person who will have it to do, and that's usually the secretary. It's not easy, either, to produce minutes of a meeting. One meeting recently lasted four and a half hours, which left me with seven sides of minutes and a lot of notes in the margin saying 'for action'; but 'for action' by whom? – again, it's usually the secretary. There's always a lot of following up to do.

I usually go on all engagements now. Competitions, concerts, recordings – everything the band does, I'm there; although this has only been in the last three years, since I retired. Before that I couldn't always go, and I used to find that if I went on an engagement nothing happened, but if I couldn't go then something would happen – not always to do with my absence, but something would go wrong.

PATRICK HOWARTH: *It sounds as if you are carrying on with a full-time job after retirement?*

KEN HIRST: I can make it into a full-time job if I want to, and I tend to do more now than I did when I was working, when I had to rely on other people, like the bandmaster, the band sergeant, the conductor or members of the committee.

PATRICK HOWARTH: *What does the band sergeant do?*

KEN HIRST: Various people have different ideas about what his responsibilities are. Basically, I suppose, he is the equivalent of a road-manager to a pop-group. He organizes the coach and says where and when it will stop, and so on.

PATRICK HOWARTH: *Will the sergeant be a member of the band?*

KEN HIRST: Usually, yes.

PATRICK HOWARTH: *Does the secretary look after finance, and how does the financial side work?*

KEN HIRST: When I first became secretary I was also treasurer, and was both for a long number of years, but I never really liked the treasurer side of the job. I could do it more easily now because I've got a computer, but I gave up the treasurer's duties about fifteen years ago. The colliery administrative officer is now band treasurer.

PATRICK HOWARTH: *Does much of the band's money come from the colliery?*

KEN HIRST: No. There's no money from the colliery, other than, I think, still a levy of a penny a week from the workforce; in years gone by that used to amount to quite a good sum, but now it's about £400 a year, which is not even worth talking about.

PATRICK HOWARTH: *How does Grimethorpe finance itself?*

KEN HIRST: From everything we get: money from concerts, prize-money from contests, fees and royalties from recordings.

PATRICK HOWARTH: *Do band members pay a subscription?*

KEN HIRST: No. I wouldn't dare attempt to charge my lads anything – they'd go up the wall!

Everything that comes in from what we do goes into the band fund, and our players do not receive fees for playing those engagements, unlike some of the top bands in the country. I may be wrong, but I think Black Dyke usually share up the whole fee between them, while the firm possibly settles the expenses, which means that the players get a fair sum for every date they play. The Grimethorpe bandsmen just get three or four pounds for turning out to a concert, which might cover the beer money – I wouldn't like to say! If we go somewhere where we need to eat, we book a meal, or if we need to stay over, we book hotels; when we go down to London for a few days we pay the band a meal allowance, which is quite good but not excessive. But for playing a concert they won't get much. We like to say that they are looked after at the colliery, and that has to take care of the payment side even when we do engagements.

PATRICK HOWARTH: *Do you buy instruments out of the band fund?*

KEN HIRST: All the instruments since 1968 have been bought by the band, but in ones or twos rather than a complete set. It would be nice still to be able to buy a complete set of instruments for £3,250, as you could twenty years ago. I think you'd have to put at least one nought on the end these days.

PATRICK HOWARTH: *What is the role of the pit and its relationship to the band nowadays? Most of the band work there, which is quite uncommon, I believe?*

KEN HIRST: Yes, it is, and it's becoming a bit of a problem as far as we are concerned. You see, most of the bands in the country are not connected to a colliery or a factory, or to anything, in fact, and so they are not responsible for finding their members employment. Today, as you know, keeping yourself in full-time employment is a big problem, especially with so many others looking for jobs as well. So it's difficult to maintain a hundred per cent of our players in jobs at the colliery – but we've still got nineteen members working there out of twenty-seven, which is pretty good.

PATRICK HOWARTH: *I believe no one at Black Dyke works for Foster's any more?*

KEN HIRST: No, but Dyke are a little different from us, because although they have no one working at the mill, they have always had the enviable name in brass banding. No matter what we all choose to say about Black Dyke, at the end of the day they have virtually been the best there is and continue in that tradition now. Black Dyke is always a band to fear in competition; to win anything you have to beat Black Dyke, and they are always the band you think about first. Over the years you've had bands like Foden's, or Fairey's, or Besses o' th' Barn, but over all the others there has always been Black Dyke. I think we are all envious of the reputation Black

Dyke has had in the past and still has. Because of this, players from all over the country, but especially Yorkshire, want to play in Black Dyke, so they never seem to have any difficulty filling positions. The added attraction is that they pay their players quite a lucrative fee for playing engagements.

PATRICK HOWARTH: *Do Foster's continue to support the band?*

KEN HIRST: Foster's support the band because it is a good advertisement for the firm – their name gets mentioned everywhere the band goes, so they continue to put money into it. The only way we can compare to Black Dyke is that we have the support of the colliery, because the biggest proportion of our players is employed there. But apart from Grimethorpe and Dyke you also have bands with sponsorship – it's getting a bit like football teams. Wingates, who used to be Wingates Temperance, are now British Aerospace; Foden's Motor Works no longer support the band, but it has kept the name and is now the Britannia Building Society Foden Band! Desford Colliery was originally a mining band, but that colliery hasn't existed for a good number of years and the band has been known as Desford Colliery Dowty Band for some time. A lot of the top bands are sponsored by somebody – OK, sponsorship can be something very small, but it can run to something very, very big. I would think that some bands get thirty to forty thousand a year from sponsors. I don't really know what anyone gets, but a firm like John Foster's must put in something like that, otherwise they couldn't afford to cover the expenses and pay the players as well as they do.

It's getting increasingly difficult for us to compete with bands that are getting sponsorship, because they are possibly able to offer more than we can. If we can't offer jobs any more, then we are almost getting to the stage of calling ourselves a public subscription band, where we have no means of support other than the public in our area.

PATRICK HOWARTH: *Like Brighouse and Rastrick?*

KEN HIRST: Yes. Brighouse you could probably call a public subscription band, although they are slightly different from us and Black Dyke. They have a very big building in Brighouse which they use as their band room for rehearsals, and they hire it out to people for dancing classes and things like that, so they have a fair amount of income from their building. Also, of course, they were fairly successful in the hit-parade with 'The Floral Dance', and they earned quite a lot of money from that. I didn't want us to be famous for playing something like 'The Floral Dance', but I was still envious because of all the money they made out of it. Money is what you need all the time to do what you want to do; to keep yourselves up to date with good uniforms, dress uniforms or walking-out uniforms or whatever, to be able to replace instruments, keep the band room in good order – it all takes finance.

PATRICK HOWARTH: *How does the recruitment of new players and the booking of conductors work? Is that done by the committee?*

KEN HIRST: With regard to auditions, the committee

may advertise that there is a vacant chair in the band. However, we don't do a lot of advertising, because we've usually got a player in mind who we know is interested in coming to Grimethorpe and we will approach him verbally. Lower-section bands call this poaching, but that's nonsense, really – if you get in touch with a player in another band to ask him if he is interested in coming to Grimethorpe, and if he says yes, passes an audition and is offered the job, you don't sling a chain round his neck and drag him to Grimethorpe, because if he doesn't want to come he stops where he is; how can that be poaching? In recent years I haven't heard that much about it, but in years gone by if you took a player from another band you were always accused of poaching.

PATRICK HOWARTH: *Who decides on which conductors to book?*

KEN HIRST: Usually it's the band – they have a discussion among the full band and decide who they want to try. Once they've decided, they draw up a short-list and get in touch with the conductors to ask them if they are interested. Not that they always know who they want – in fact, we've had more conductors than the National Bus Company!

PATRICK HOWARTH: *Has your job changed as Grimethorpe has become more famous and successful?*

KEN HIRST: I suppose my job as secretary has increased as greater success and fame have come along. Up until 1972, when your father came to the band, we liked to think that we had a fairly successful band, and in terms of competition results I suppose we had. But for the early years of my time as secretary the function of the band, by and large, was to give summer concerts in the parks around the country. We always seemed to be playing out of doors, and a lot of people, especially the general public, seem to think that that is the only place to listen to a brass band – in the open air. But I would say that the only place to listen to music of any kind is in the concert hall. So in days gone by I would send out a lot of letters to local authorities, asking them if they were interested in booking the Grimethorpe Colliery Band. I haven't done anything like that for donkey's years, though. I wouldn't dream of it. There was a changeover which came about nearly twenty years ago, when the top bands stopped playing in parks and most of their jobs became concerts in proper concert halls; most of the work changed from the summer to the winter. After 1972 the summer was often taken up with foreign tours, which created a lot of new work for me. In the last twenty years my job has increased maybe tenfold as the nature of the band's work has changed.

PATRICK HOWARTH: *Has your computer helped to make the workload more bearable?*

KEN HIRST: It has and it hasn't. I'd always been interested in getting a computer of some kind, even before I'd finished working. When I did retire I had a bit of money, so I bought a Sanyo small business computer with a printer, which had a word-processing package and a spreadsheet and so on. One of the first things I did was to build up a database of the music library.

But I had some difficulty with the software for the Sanyo, which held me back from really getting the most out of it. Then I won a Compaq computer from the BBC2 programme *Micro Live,* which had Lotus Symphony software as part of the prize.

PATRICK HOWARTH: *What was the prize for?*

KEN HIRST: There was a competition relating to an integrated software package – the Lotus Symphony – which had word-processing, spreadsheets, database, graphics and communication in a single package. The idea of the competition was to think of applications for this package, which seemed to me an ideal way of organizing the band's business. I was put on to a short-list of seven and a week later I got a phone call to say that I was one of the three winners. Apparently there had been between seven and eight hundred entries. The daft thing about it was that when I decided to send my entry in, I addressed it to Thames Television, and Thames passed it on to the producer of BBC2's *Micro Live;* otherwise I wouldn't have stood a chance, because I'd sent it to the wrong firm! Anyway, I won the Compaq Twin Disk Computer which had been upgraded to 640K memory, which was more than enough to take the Symphony software. There was also an Epson 15-inch printer, the software itself, and three days' training down in Windsor.

PATRICK HOWARTH: *Do you use it for all the band's business?*

KEN HIRST: Everything I do with the band I do on the computer. I find the word-processing program very useful, so I can use it as a typewriter. It is much faster than a manual typewriter, of course, so I'm able to work more quickly, but the disadvantage is that, as a result, I seem to produce more words than I used to. The music library with the Lotus Symphony software is what I call 'idiot-proof': it's much easier to use than the one on the Sanyo. I've got about two thousand pieces of music on one disk and plenty of room for more. I've got it programmed to give me a list numerically and alphabetically – so if I want a list of pieces composed by Beethoven I just give it the right command and it will print it out for me, according to my references; if I want a list of all our overtures, it will do exactly the same. So at any time I can run off a completely new list for the librarian, which is easily updated when we get new material.

PATRICK HOWARTH: *Have any of the other bands started using a computer, do you know?*

KEN HIRST: I haven't heard of anyone else. Among the top bands, I think I'm the person well known for working on a computer. Certainly everyone seems to know about it. I've had a few telephone calls about it; the manager of the Jim Shepherd Versatile Brass was interested. I remember one man phoned me up and said, 'I understand you've got all your music on a computer.' 'That's right,' I said. But then he asked me: 'How do you go about changing a part if you need to?' I didn't know what he was talking about at first, because what I've got is just a database of the pieces we have in our music library. He thought I had on computer every piece we've got in the library – the crotchets, the quavers, the lot! Where he got that idea from, I don't know. You wouldn't need a microcomputer; you'd need one of those mainframe things. He must have been a proper idiot. It's a nice idea, and I suppose someone will come up with a package that will do it one day.

PATRICK HOWARTH: *Can we talk about contests now? What is your role when the band is at a competition?*

KEN HIRST: Usually the first thing we do is to make for the place where we've arranged to rehearse on the day – it's not really a rehearsal, it's more just to get the players blown in; if you can't play the thing on the day of the competition, you may as well stop at home anyway. From there I usually go to the draw; that is, if it's not pre-drawn. At places like the Open Championship it's a bit nerve-racking. You go into a room and there's a representative for each band; somebody draws out the number of a band on the programme, then the representative of that band draws a ball or a disc out of another bag and that's the number where your band will play. On quite a few occasions I can remember sitting there and my number has been the one left in the bag at the end, so I haven't drawn. You are always waiting for someone to draw the dreaded number one, of course. At the first Open Championship I went to draw what has since become the number I've drawn more times than any other, number two. OK, I'm lucky enough not to get number one, but I've drawn a lot of number twos.

PATRICK HOWARTH: *What happens after the draw?*

KEN HIRST: I go back to the rehearsal room and tell them what number they are playing at, and it's decided from that what time we'll leave the rehearsal room; whether we'll go away for a time, if we've got a late draw, before meeting again for another little tootle and then going off to the contest hall. I suppose I have to decide what I'm going to do for the duration of the competition – recently I've only listened to one band during contests, and that's my own. Years and years ago I used to listen to eleven or twelve of the fancied outfits, but would then feel very disgruntled when I heard the results, so now I only listen to Grimethorpe. If I think we've played well, then that's it; I'm not really interested in hearing the others.

In any case, if it's a competition where everyone's playing the same piece, no one has the same interpretation; in fact, some of the performances sound like different pieces altogether. I find contest days to be very time-consuming, very boring affairs. Particularly if you play early, you are just standing around waiting for the other bands to play and the judges to come out of their box and give the results. I think it would be much better if it was like ice-skating and you were given your points immediately after your performance, so that if somebody had already beaten you, you could get on the bus and go home if you liked.

I don't like competitions very much; the set-piece competitions I don't like at all. I think what we're doing is spending a lot of time rehearsing a piece which, more often than not, we'll never play again. We're spending a lot of money hiring a professional conductor, and a lot of time rehearsing every night during the weeks before the contest. I think the time spent trying to win a contest would be far better spent preparing the pieces for concerts, which are for entertaining the public.

I must say I do like these 'entertainment' competitions, where everybody plays a programme of their own choice. From the audience's point of view they are interesting: there's a lot more in them, they aren't boring. OK, you are still standing around all day, but if I go in to hear another band's programme I don't find it as boring as listening to the same piece again. So I do like the entertainment contests, but I suppose that may be partly because over the years Grimethorpe has been more successful than anyone else at them. I don't like the set-piece competitions at all; they are a rat race from start to finish. The outcome invariably depends on who the organizers put in the adjudicators' box, and I feel the results are often due to some queer ideas. It's always this notion of interpretation. Obviously every man who conducts has a different idea about how a piece should be played, but I can't see why that should have any bearing on the final result of a competition. The only criterion that the judges should apply is perfection of playing: if one band plays the piece better than any other, then that band should win. If two bands play the piece equally well, then bring interpretation into it, and if one of the two bands plays it as the judges like it to be played, then that band will win – fair enough. But I don't think that the judges should impose their interpretation on every band that plays. A lot of the judges who appear at these contests are not really fit to judge some of the conductors of some of the brass bands, anyway. If the judges come from the brass band world, at a big contest like the Open, all the best conductors will be conducting their own bands, and they will be being judged by lesser conductors.

PATRICK HOWARTH: *You mentioned foreign tours earlier. What part do you play in the organization and running of these?*

KEN HIRST: Before we go on tour the main thing I have to do is prepare a thing called a 'carnet', which is a list of everything we are taking with us – all the instruments and baggage. You have to apply to the local Chamber of Commerce, who stamp the carnet and give you enough copies for all the various customs posts you have to go through. Every customs point must stamp your carnet, otherwise you have trouble bringing the stuff back into the country. I remember in Italy we had virtually to threaten them to get the thing stamped – they would have let us take anything in.

It's very difficult, because you try to get everything on to your list and then someone says 'We're not taking that, we're taking this.' But once it's stamped you can't change it. I did once, and of course the minute we went through customs they went straight for whatever it was I'd changed.

Before we set off I have to try to make a proper itinerary of everything, so everyone knows what we are doing.

PATRICK HOWARTH: *Do you deal with hotel bookings?*

KEN HIRST: No, the people connected with the tour normally do that. I've never been in charge of booking the hotels; if I had, some would have been blown up! We have tried to insist on this or that class of hotel, but it hasn't always been satisfactory. We had some real sparklers in France, but some were absolute disasters – one of our lads had a room where he could see the stars through the ceiling. We took photographs so we had some evidence for when we got back home.

PATRICK HOWARTH: *Does the band enjoy the tours?*

KEN HIRST: Yes, I think the lads do enjoy them. They tend to complain about them before we go, but if I went down to the band room and said that we were going to America for three weeks, they'd all be clapping their hands, they'd all want to go.

PATRICK HOWARTH: *Since the tours take the place of a holiday, do you ever get much of a holiday out of them?*

KEN HIRST: Yes, I think you can enjoy yourself as well as having a job of work to do, although you always have to be thinking about what's happening the next day, and so on.

The best tour I've been on from that point of view was Australia. We had a tour manager, Tony Reagan, who organized everything down to the last little detail, wherever we went, and we travelled a lot in Australia. We took off and landed twenty-two times, apart from arriving in and leaving the country, and each time everyone had to have a seat and a ticket, and Tony organized it all; I just sat back and watched. The only time I had any problems was with individual players getting upset.

Other tours haven't been so good; the

organizers could be a bit naughty. The first tour we went on, when your father took us to America for the Bicentennial, we had a courier who was supposed to see to everything, but things went wrong. I remember the organizer muddled up a massed band concert we were to do with Cory; no one knew it was on, although we'd rehearsed the two bands together for it. Things like that cause trouble, but if we have a good courier I haven't got too much to worry about, apart from the checking of all our tackle. We always take someone with us to look after the equipment – usually Bob Davidson, who's over seventy now, but we call him our porter.

PATRICK HOWARTH: *Looking back on thirty-three years of banding, is there one particular moment that sticks in your mind?*

KEN HIRST: It's very difficult to decide. I've been present at competitions or concerts where I've thought the band has played really well; out of this world, even. I can think of performances conducted by your father, which haven't in the end won competitions when I've thought we've walked it. I can think of quite a few instances like that. But I think the main thing was in 1963, when we were due to play in the Yorkshire Regional Qualifying Competition, which qualified you to go to London, and the test-piece was the *Rienzi* Overture by Wagner. I can't remember who arranged the piece or who the judge was, but I do know that all the bands in Yorkshire were there – Black Dyke, Brighouse and so on – nobody had byes. I can remember going right back to the top of the hall, 'the gods', where the bandsmen sat, and listening to our performance. The band started and I thought 'This sounds good', and I could see the other bandsmen saying to each other 'This sounds good.' When they got to the end of the piece, I don't know why, but I knew that we had won. I didn't give a damn who the judge was, or how the other bands played, I just knew that we'd won. I went from the top of the St George's Hall down to the bottom, where the band room was, and I shook hands with every member of the band. I've never seen myself so excited in all my life, because I'm not that type of person – I don't get hilarious about anything, I just take everything as it comes. But that day I just knew, and when the results came out, we had won. I've heard a lot of outstanding performances, as I said, but I've never felt like that, before or since.

PATRICK HOWARTH: *Have you any ambitions left for yourself and the band?*

KEN HIRST: I should like to do some more tours abroad if possible. I think what we've done as a band since 1972 has been far more than we could ever have dreamed about. Before 1972, to my way of thinking, compared with after was just ordinary. OK, your father has brought us some contemporary music, avant-garde music, and he always knows what I feel about it; invariably I've told him I think it's awful! But what I've always said is that it's a challenge to the players in the band, and so they are more able to play some of the other stuff, which is more listenable, if you like. We are noted for playing that sort of music – if someone wants an avant-garde piece performed, the first band they think of is Grimethorpe, so it has done some good. I think the lads like playing it to a certain degree, but I think they are a little embarrassed if some members of the audience are not expecting that sort of thing, which has happened on occasions.

But of all the things that have happened since 1972, it's the tours that stand out for me. Before then we'd never even been abroad; not even to Holland or Belgium, as other bands had. So I should like to do more tours.

6

Waltz

Elgar Howarth on the Traditional Repertoire

BRASS BANDS OR SO the general public used to think and the popular press still thinks, play tiddly-om-pom-pom: oompah music for the pier, promenade and park. *Marching and Waltzing,* for instance, used to be until fairly recently the title of a BBC radio programme, the marches played by a band, the waltzes by a BBC staff light orchestra, the lighter the fare the better[1].

Certainly the old traditional repertoire was not, is not, highbrow. Programmes of band music are normally aimed primarily at entertainment, not cultural or spiritual uplift (though the Salvation Army will demur), and there are many who would argue that they are none the worse for that. The very sound of a fine band in good form, they would say, is uplifting in itself; and so it can be, but sound should be the servant of repertoire, not vice versa.

Yet it must be said that neither is the traditional repertoire entirely low-brow – far from it, as we shall see as we examine the music with which bands made, and to some extent still maintain, their concert-giving reputation. Cloth-cap, their image has been called, a term deeply resented by most bands and their followers, but it should be an honourable title, since there is many a good pair of ears and a keen musical intelligence beneath such headgear.

The old repertoire indeed, as it was first established, represented the working man's appreciation of the wider musical world available to him as conductor, arranger, instrumentalist and listener, at a time when opportunities to hear the original article were pretty rare, even for more

---

1 This is not to denigrate the BBC, which in other ways has done more than any to promote serious band music.

affluent folk. It is a tribute to his taste that he chose so much that was excellent and modelled his style of performance on elegance rather than stridency.

The rather curious format of this book is based on a programme played some thirty years ago by a band in a park; the band, as it happens, that I was brought up in, Barton Hall Works Band from Patricroft, Manchester. It illustrates the kind of repertoire bands played in this period, and conforms in most ways to the formula from which most programmes were constructed at that time; though not entirely, since the conductor, my father, had slightly unusual ideas for his generation. A more usual shape for the programme would have been to start with a march (to warm up) or a popular overture, frequently both, followed by a cornet solo, a medley of traditional tunes, perhaps, a 'novelty' item of sorts or a waltz, 'gems' from a great composer – Weber, Tchaikovsky, Beethoven, say – or from a popular musical comedy – Gilbert and Sullivan, maybe – and so to the interval. After the break the pattern is more or less repeated, maybe with two solos – trombone or euphonium – and a rousing rhapsody to close. Most items were no longer than six or seven minutes unless, rather unusually, a contest piece was included, which was some-times done, especially if the band had been recently successful in a competition. Test-pieces, however, might be ten to twelve minutes long and were generally thought to be over-taxing for weekend entertainment.

The Barton Hall programme is a little more adventurous, including as it does a xylophone solo and a vocalist; he, not a member of the band, also acted as compère. Where it differs again from convention, not in style of music but in repertoire, is in its reliance on arrangements done by my father. An older tradition had seen much transcribing for bands done by many famous arrangers from the turn of the century onwards – William Rimmer, J. A. Greenwood, Harold Round, for instance, many of whose arrangements had been published for the availability of bands in general, and, naturally, for the financial benefit of the authors.

By the middle of the century most bands had come to rely almost exclusively on these standards (opera or operetta

selections by and large, plus a deluge of popular light pieces
of the time – Ketèlbey, Heyken, Sullivan), with a conse-
quent loss of a personal touch; that is, arrangements done
for an individual band. My father was a throwback to
that earlier period of conductor-arranger. Our tiny living-
room was a constant scene of chaos as he sat surrounded by
manuscript parts, endlessly and happily arranging Neapoli-
tan airs, Beethoven symphonies, Haydn occasional pieces
and the odd Italian march.

Here was tiddly-om-pom-pom in a more serious vein,
giving to his band a kind of special pride in a repertoire only
they possessed. Brass bands are tribal and such exclusivity
was highly valued. Today the same sense still exists at bands
like Black Dyke Mills or Besses o' th' Barn, whose libraries
include what are often the only extant copies of arrangements by Alexander Owen, one of their former conductors.
The pieces rarely see the light of day, but are jealously
guarded special property – 'gems' from *Tristan und Isolde,
Die Walküre,* and so on. Owen seems, in the matter of
repertoire, to have been rather ahead of his time, as does
John Greenwood, who arranged 'selections' from Elgar's
two symphonies.

These items by Wagner and Elgar are obviously a world
apart from oompah, and demonstrate an ambitious, if
sometimes rather naïve, belief in the possibilities of transcription for band; and in any case they were not 'repertoire'
in the general sense. For one thing, their virtuosic difficulties
preclude, even today, performances by any but the top five
or six bands.

The general repertoire was simpler, standard and fairly
fixed, it seemed, by the time Barton Mills was performing
some forty years ago, interesting for the players to rehearse
and perform, and entertaining perhaps for their keen but
dwindling fans; dull, even dire, to a general public whose
taste was changing. However, some of this traditional
repertoire still wore well, since the quality of some of the
music was much higher than is usually realized. Let us
examine the 'formula' programme in detail.

The ubiquitous march ought to have become a deadening
cliché. Continental bands, with several notable exceptions,

had got musically little further than this particular form of oompah, but the competitive British solved the problem by inventing the contest march. It is clear from the briefest observation of brass bands that their raison d'être is competition, and to compete and win in the multitude of such contests bands needed special, musically superior pieces. It is, or should be, one of the great sources of pride of British bands that they possess so many wonderful marches, less military in style than the continental type, less bombastic, though often less cheery, than Sousa, altogether more refined in style than one would expect from such home-grown, self-taught talent, often subtle in harmony and phrase length. There is an article to be written here by some A level music student or wandering American scholar, but let me offer a brief selection.

William Rimmer had a genius for the form: 'Ravenswood' is elegant, very slightly melancholy, in spite of its major key; 'Punchinello' is a great favourite, with a swaggering bass theme and a swinging trio. There are many more from the same pen. J. Ord Hume's 'BB and CF' (named after the journal *British Bandsman and Contest Field*) is a superb march; his 'Brilliant' is almost a personal favourite, but there are others. Shipley Douglas's curious 'Mephistopheles' has more tunes than can safely be packed into five minutes, but is still a winner. There is Anderson's dainty melody 'ORB' (Oldham Rifle Brigade, I believe) and Greenwood's 'Cossack', throat-catching in its minor-key memories of the great Foden Band. George Allan's 'Knights Templar' was made famous by Black Dyke Mills, whose favourite it is for the Whit Friday competition (Allan above them all, perhaps, is a study in the creative power of the self-taught amateur; he played the baritone in a band in County Durham). Maurice Johnstone, former head of music at BBC Manchester, provided two pieces of the highest order, 'Pennine Way' and 'County Palatine'. Here was early original music for brass band which has not been equalled since in this particular form.

The overtures were international in their popularity and origin, and many were expertly arranged by a host of enthusiasts eager to provide brilliant yet lyrical openings to concerts. Many sound superb in their new brass orchestration: Rossini's 'William Tell' (lyrical euphonium, virtuoso cornet), 'The Italian Girl in Algiers', 'The Barber of Seville', 'The Thievish Magpie', all played often; Suppé's 'Poet and Peasant' (horn – not cello – solo and cadenza), 'Light Cavalry', 'Morning, Noon and Night in Vienna'; Hérold's 'Zampa' and Auber's 'The Bronze Horse', both nearly forgotten in the orchestral repertoire; Thomas' 'Raymond' (wonderful cornet part); and of course Verdi's 'Sicilian Vespers' and, relatively recently, 'The Force of Destiny'.

And many more . . .It was here, and in the related music of the operatic selections, that the foundations of the lyrical style of playing which is so peculiar to British bands were laid. The charm of this music relies very much on a light touch; and cornet players, particularly, had to find a beauty of sound and variety of tonguing techniques, a dexterity of fingers and a subtlety of musical expression to cope with these nineteenth-century melodies, reliant as they normally are on the violin, the woodwind, and especially the voice. That they did so, making the music valid for purely brass formations, is evident in the enthusiasm expressed by Elgar and Holst when they eventually were invited to write for band; one of the rewards of this repertoire, in fact, was the self-confidence gained, with which bands approached the newer repertoire when it arrived on the contest scene.

The cornet solo came early in the programme, for reasons of stamina. The smaller the mouthpiece, the greater the tension in the embouchure and the sooner fatigue sets in. Enjoying, therefore, this early spot in the proceedings, cornet soloists were able to demonstrate their often considerable technical and musical skills. The Air varié, a tune with normally about four or five variations, was (and still is) very popular. A number of virtuosi, international in reputation and origin – John Hartmann, Paris Chambers, Jean-Baptiste Arban – had written pieces of a similar pattern: introduction (cantabile), tune (well known), first variation (showy), second variation (very showy), third variation (impossible!), fourth variation (slow: minor key), fifth variation (polacca or triple-tongued toccata). 'The Carnival of Venice' was a great favourite with arrangers and soloists alike, but 'Rule Britannia', 'Weber's Last Waltz', 'Mermaid Song', 'My love is like a red, red rose' and 'Facilità' were close behind.

A newer form of solo was the Polka or Caprice, which might have the form: introduction, tune A, tune B, tune C, (maybe D,) back to A and a coda; this became very successful, too, rivalling the Air varié. The music was original and at its best was good salon stuff. Demare's 'Cleopatra' was widely played, as was Percy Code's 'Zelda'; a novelty was Windsor's 'Alpine Echoes', featuring the 'echo' cornet, which had a built-in instant muting possibility. This last piece was made particularly famous by its performance on record by Harry Mortimer, the greatest of the lyrical cornet players, with his band, Foden's. These solos were of course taken up by other instruments, especially the euphonium, whose popularity rivals that of the cornet, just as the cello does the violin. The trombone had a different set of pieces, again written by various virtuosi, most of which featured the glissando, the great comic cliché effect of a noble instrument – 'The Acrobat', 'The Joy Wheel', 'The Firefly', 'The Slippery Slide' (enough said!) and, most hated by me and my brother, who was unfortunate enough to have to play it, 'Barnacle Bill'. All these are still played, since strangely, though band music has moved on, the solo repertoire has been slower to develop. The same applies to the 'slow melody' repertoire, as it is called. In band concerts slow tunes were often played as an encore to a solo (unless a duet was favoured) and this repertoire was much in demand at the many 'slow melody' competitions; for example: 'Bless this house', 'The Holy City', 'The Lost Chord' – many popular Victorian or Edwardian ballads, in fact – 'A brown bird singing', 'I hear you calling me' or, with a slightly different flavour, 'Softly awakes my heart' from Saint-Saëns' *Samson and Delilah,* or 'Solveig's Song' from Grieg's *Peer Gynt.*

The waltzes were frankly popular items, regarded as 'fillers' between solo and grand selection. Waldteufel, Ancliffe, Lehár, Strauss and others all vied for inclusion here, with 'Gold and Silver', 'Nights of Gladness', 'The Skaters' Waltz', 'Estudiantina', as well as 'The Blue

Danube', being high on the list.

The operatic selections, like their companion pieces the overtures, gave a special quality to the repertoire. Vocal style was admired as a model for soloists particularly, and the 'grand selections' from *Il trovatore, La traviata, Cavalleria rusticana* and *Pagliacci* provided a wealth of Italianate melody which helped to identify band style. Nor were the Italian masters alone – 'Weber's Works' I remember as staple musical fare, with items from *Der Freischütz* and *Oberon* included in it; and 'Beethoven's Works' too, with pieces even from the solo piano repertoire arranged for full band. Tchaikovsky was not so common, though the *1812* overture was and remains the favourite 'finisher', but ballet music of Gounod *(Faust)* and Rossini *(William Tell)* was a staunch standby. This type of music was, of course, already old-fashioned to some bandsmen and conductors; it was thirty, forty, sometimes fifty years since the arrangements had been made, and bands were as conscious then, as now, of image and of the need to keep up to date with current taste.

Musical comedy seemed to be part of the answer. Gilbert and Sullivan, better known to the general public than Mascagni or Weber, was played often, since most British audiences of the time knew the most popular tunes, but Lionel Monckton's *The Arcadians*, Sigmund Romberg's *Desert Song*, Franz Lehár's *Merry Widow* and Richard Tauber's *Old Chelsea* were all familiar, too. Ivor Novello was up to date, and his shows all smash hits – bands wallowed in 'We'll gather lilacs' and in the tunes from *The Dancing Years* and *King's Rhapsody*. American musicals were the coming thing, of course, with a stronger rhythmic sense in general than their British and European counterparts. They were thought to be very modern and in conservative circles rather dangerous, their syncopations lying too close to jazz for comfort, for, strangely, the brass band has never been at home with jazz style. The public, however, welcomed *Show Boat*, a golden oldie, *Oklahoma!*, *Carousel*, *Annie Get Your Gun* and *South Pacific*.

The last ingredient in the formula was what one might call the 'strong finisher'. As already mentioned, Tchaikovsky's

1812 overture was a prime choice, but so too were the Slavonic Rhapsodies of the little-known Viennese Carl Friedmann – wild, gypsy-like stuff, crammed with semiquavers and quivering vibrato-full rubati. There were other solutions. 'Nightfall in Camp', complete with bugle calls, might be a suitable close for a Sunday evening park job; or it might be a frankly religioso 'meditation' based on a hymn tune – but usually it was fireworks or the circus, and the grandiose effect of the Prelude to Act III of *Lohengrin* thrown in for good measure.

This near-fossilized, creaking concert repertoire, containing much that was good, but stale, which was undoubtedly loved by the band public, but viewed with disdain by younger audiences and the wider musical world, was existing side by side with another tradition, the contest test-piece, and that repertoire was developing in a significantly different way.

The two major championships – the British Open held at Belle Vue, Manchester, in September, an invitation event; and the National Championship, held originally at the Crystal Palace and later at the Royal Albert Hall, London, in October, a qualifying event – had both in their early days been in step with concert-giving, relying entirely on arrangements of excerpts from the great masters: Spohr, Gounod, Verdi, Rossini, Donizetti, Wagner, Weber, Mendelssohn and so on, mostly operatic selections or 'gems' from oratorio.

In 1913 John Henry Iles, contest owner and organizer of the National, decided to break with this tradition and to commission a piece of original music for band as a test-piece for his contest. 'Labour and Love' by Percy Fletcher was the first of a succession of new works for band, some by the leading composers of the time, ordered for the National by Iles, a man of obvious vision and faith in his chosen musical medium.

Many of the early originals remain favourites today, especially 'Life Divine' by Cyril Jenkins, written in 1921, a rhetorical tone-poem in full-blown romantic style, replete with ardent sequences and Lisztian harmony. Holst's beautiful 'Moorside Suite' of 1928, though respected, has sadly not won as many hearts, and neither has Elgar's 'Severn Suite' of 1930, though John Ireland's 'Downland Suite' (1932) and 'Comedy Overture' (1934) have proved popular.

When Iles took over the rival firm in Manchester in 1925 he instigated a similar policy. From 1925 to 1928 he commissioned test-pieces from Thomas Keighley, a composer who taught at the Royal Manchester College of Music. Keighley provided a Shakespearian quartet: 'Macbeth' in 1925, 'A Midsummer Night's Dream' (1926), 'The Merry Wives of Windsor' (1927) and 'Lorenzo' (a character in *The Merchant of Venice*) in 1928. To the best of my knowledge the first three are now never played, but 'Lorenzo' still has an occasional outing, and rightly so – it is loosely constructed and a bit too pomposo, but it has some lovely tunes and is very imaginatively scored. It must have helped convince the northern audience, and original pieces now caught on – Granville Bantock wrote 'Oriental Rhapsody' for Manchester in 1930 and 'Prometheus Unbound', a fine if elusive work, for London in 1933. Herbert Howells, sometimes thought austere, produced the brilliant 'Pageantry' for Manchester in 1934, a vintage year, as London heard Ireland's 'Comedy Overture' for the first time.

Here was high adventure, original music for brass band often marvellously imagined and beautifully scored, providing not only technical challenge for contest purposes but also a new repertoire of serious, musically signifiant pieces specially conceived for the medium. Iles's inspiration, in fact, caused a dozen or so first-class scores to be written in a golden age between, say, 1920 and the outbreak of war in 1939, and several other pieces of real merit, too. It was a new world not just for players and audiences but for conductors as well. The old selections were obviously weak in construction, one aria or chorus following another, linked sometimes by crude bridge passages and uneasy modulations. The better of the new pieces gave challenges to the musicality of the conductors which they had not faced before, since they now had to shape not just melodic line and accompaniment, difficult enough indeed, but development sections (where musical ideas get argued out) and recapitulations (where tunes return, often with fresh significance and added weight of thought).

The new pieces brought new harmony, too. Harry Mortimer recounts how he, his father Fred and brother Alex visited the film *Things to Come* several times to familiarize themselves with the style of Arthur Bliss, who had written the score for the film and the brand-new 'Kenilworth' for the National. A fresh interest was aroused in the musical world in general by the bands' investment in these new works. 'Corno di Bassetto' – George Bernard Shaw, no less – visited the Crystal Palace to hear the championships and liked what he heard: style and content were at last being married, the bands seemed on their way out of the doldrums, advancing away from the cloth cap they despised towards the musical respectability they craved.

Hitler intervened. The National was abandoned in 1939 for the duration of the war. The Open bravely struggled on, sometimes with original music but sometimes slipping back to the old arrangement formula. Some of the best players, after all, were otherwise occupied.

After the war, for various reasons, the system changed. 'Home-grown' composers were preferred to the bigger names of the ordinary musical establishment, sometimes with excellent results and sometimes not. Throughout the 1950s and 1960s a certain cosiness crept into the contest repertoire, for though Vaughan Williams, Bantock and Howells all produced interesting works for the National, and Gilbert Vinter a much-needed taste of (very mild) modernity with his 'Variations on a Ninth' (1964), 'Triumphant Rhapsody' (1965) and 'Spectrum' (1969 – this last for the Open), the arrangements often crept back in, to the delight of the fans but the detriment of development in the original repertoire. The Open, meanwhile, favoured the tone-poems of Eric Ball, who has written extensively and adeptly for bands both in the secular world and the Salvation Army. His 'Resurgam' (1950) is arguably the most popular piece of original music with older band enthusiasts. Richly scored, *in modo religioso*, it seemed to give band composers a self-confidence which had not been in evidence before.

Strangely enough, the exclusion of these pieces from the concert repertoire was almost total; as suggested before, they were considered too 'heavy', or too formal, perhaps, for the rather matey atmosphere of the average band concert. A test-piece was a test-piece, and best left at that, or so it was thought.

By the 1970s a worrying situation had developed, since bands seemed to be losing what public appeal they still had. Local authorities found them less interesting to hire for the old proven venues of pier and park, and young players found a multitude of other musical possibilities being offered to them in youth orchestras or big bands. The excitement of the contest was still a big pull to players and fans alike, but the bands, though regarded with a certain nostalgic affection, seemed to many to be even further out of touch with the ordinary music world than ever, and this in spite of continuing (even, in my view, improving) high standards of performance, at least among the leading bands.

Except for the diehards, many in the movement expressed a need for a new image, for change, but were uncertain what direction this ought to take. To outsiders it was obvious that part of the problem was the repertoire and the programming; in the 1970s a fresh approach was needed.

Serenade

1970–Today

WHILE THE 1960s was a period of consolidation and little progress one major change did take place in the later years of the decade which was to help widen the musical scope of brass banding. During the 1930s orchestral and military band brass instruments had changed to low pitch, as had all other musical instruments. Brass bands, however, had stubbornly stuck to the old high pitch, thereby isolating themselves from all other musicians except choristers. This attitude had economic as well as musical implications, because manufacturers had to run two production lines in order to produce the two types of instrument. As labour costs rose in the 1960s this diversity became uneconomic, and the manufacturers began to try to persuade bandsmen to adopt the low pitch. Change has never been willingly accepted in banding, although it is only fair to point out that many smaller bands would have had difficulty in affording the cost of conversion, and even the top bands could not easily afford a brand-new set of instruments. Eventually the change was forced on the bands when, in 1965, Boosey and Hawkes announced that they were shutting down their high-pitch production line. Gradually bands bought new instruments or converted their old ones, by extending the tubing. Black Dyke Mills' victory in the National of 1967, performed on a set of new low-pitch instruments, proved that a band could sound as good as before, and the new pitch was soon accepted; although even today you will still find a few diehards who insist that the high-pitch instruments produced the only genuine brass band sound.

The change of pitch may have widened banding's potential horizons, but the resistance to change was to become characteristic. Brass bands needed to get away from the cloth-cap image and to extend their repertoire, but they did not want to alienate their traditional audience by changing too much too soon. However, some people will always think that any change is a bad thing, so opposition was inevitable and, sure enough, most of the innovations of the 1970s met with resistance.

Most of the disagreement centred on some of the new repertoire which was beginning to be performed (the major pieces themselves are discussed in Chapter 9). The piece which seems to have generated the most violent reaction was Harrison Birtwistle's 'Grimethorpe Aria' (1973) – the *British Bandsman* is full of scathing and outraged letters concerning the 'musicality' of this work. However, earlier works such as Gilbert Vinter's 'Spectrum' (1969) and Robert Simpson's 'Energy' (1971), and later compositions like 'Fireworks' (Elgar Howarth, 1975) and Hans Werner Henze's 'Ragtimes and Habaneras' (1975) came in for their fair share of flak, especially since 'Spectrum', 'Energy' and 'Fireworks' were all test-pieces and therefore impinged upon the two major contests, arguably the most traditional of all spheres of brass band activity. It is not at all surprising that this 'new' music was so badly received (although it was only a vociferous minority who bitterly complained), since avant-garde music has not been welcomed with open arms by most wider musical audiences. It is difficult as well as different music, and it is to the credit of brass bands and their followers that they have learnt to accept and appreciate some of these works relatively quickly. Indeed, the brass band composers who are most popular today, especially among the younger players, are writers like Edward Gregson and Philip Sparke, whose music has introduced new ideas – although less new or extreme ideas than, for example, Birtwistle's.

Despite its initial unpopularity, the new repertoire did create interest in brass bands among people who had never seriously considered them before. In Chapter 8, Derek Bourgeois describes how he was amazed at the technique and musicianship of the bandsmen, and his reaction was typical of many people's first encounter with bands. Most of this new audience was introduced to brass bands through the wider concert opportunities which became available thanks to the new music. In 1974 Grimethorpe Colliery and Black Dyke Mills Bands were invited to perform together at the BBC Promenade Concerts. The programme contained both new music – 'Grimethorpe Aria' – and traditional repertoire – Elgar's 'Severn Suite' and Holst's 'Moorside Suite' – thereby displaying a full range of the bands' musical capabilities and traditions. Brass bands also began to feature at concerts on the South Bank in London, and at music festivals abroad and at home. Barriers were starting to be broken down. Grimethorpe's appearance at the Leeds Music Festival in 1974 was the first by a brass band in 116 years of the festival, although Leeds is the nearest major city to many of the country's leading bands. Apart from Grimethorpe Colliery and Black Dyke Mills, Besses o' th' Barn and, later, Stanshawe Band were also instrumental in widening the repertoire and audiences, performing new pieces by John McCabe, Derek Bourgeois and Howard Burrell. These 'highbrow' concerts attracted the interest of music critics in the national press, who generally regarded brass bands as beneath their or their readers' interest, and this in turn opened more minds and ears. In more recent years this higher profile for banding has varied a little as the initial furore has died down, but Black Dyke were back at the Proms in 1987 and bands have continued to reach wider audiences without alienating their original fans.

Another new direction for bands in the 1970s which also attracted new audiences and generated new repertoire was the 'entertainment' contest. This differs from the test-piece contest, such as the Open at Belle Vue or the National in London, in a number of ways. It features far fewer bands, of necessity, since each band has to present a twenty-five-minute programme, of which entertainment is as important a criterion as technical difficulty. Such criteria make great demands on the bands, who have to produce a new and exciting programme every year. The most successful bands tend to be those whose conductor can furnish them with new arrangements and compositions, which harks back to the days of Owen, Swift and Gladney, who produced a unique repertoire for their own bands. As can be imagined, a great deal of new 'light' music has been written since 1971, when the Granada Television contest, the first of the entertainment contests, was started; and if some of it has vanished without trace, much has taken its place alongside other works as a valuable part of the band repertoire. The Granada was the brainchild of Bram Gay and Granada producer Arthur Taylor, and was originally part of the Belle Vue Spring Festival; from 1982 it was held at the Spectrum centre near Warrington, and in 1987 in the Isle of Man. As usual, the contest has three adjudicators, but one sits in the open to judge the performance as visual entertainment, while the other two remain enclosed in the adjudicators' box and give their marks for musical and technical content. The Granada has become firmly established as an important part of the banding year, not least because the winners perform their winning programme on television, one of the few opportunities brass bands have to appear on this medium. The success of the Granada entertainment contest has produced a crop of similar events, most notably the Rothmans Brass in Concert Contest at Darlington. Audiences at these contests can be rather different from those at a test-piece contest. There is genuinely greater entertainment to be had from them in my view, whereas an occasion like the National is possibly more the territory of the connoisseur, who is happy to listen to twenty-two different interpretations of the same piece. Whether this is so or not, contests like the Granada and the Rothmans have introduced new fans to the excitement of a band competition and the diversity of a band concert.

Other new contests were founded during the 1970s, but they tended to be based on the test-piece formula of the National or Open. Some of them, such as the Wills Contest, did not survive for very long: although it was enthusiastically supported by the bands, the sponsors decided to withdraw their support and the contest died. The Pontin's contests, on the other hand, have been very successful, attracting a large number of entries and large crowds to the finals, which are held in holiday camps during November. The rival holiday camp company, Butlin's, has also sponsored a contest, the Butlin's Youth Brass Band Championship of Great Britain, which has become a very popular part of the National Festival at the Royal Albert Hall in October.

If interest in brass bands was increasing during the mid-1970s, it still tended to be limited to those who might have some connection with bands (albeit a tenuous connection in many cases) or to those who were interested in hearing the new music that bands had begun to perform. To most people in Britain a brass band was still something that played in parks on Sundays and, in an age of television, pop music and cinema, an old-fashioned irrelevance. Unfortunately, the event which brought bands to the wider public eye confirmed rather than dispelled this image. In 1976 Brighouse and Rastrick Band had released a 45 rpm single of the old tune 'The Floral Dance', to no reaction whatsoever. Gradually, however, Radio 2 had picked up on the record and requests for it began to flood in. By the end of 1977 it was at number two in the charts and sold over 700,000 copies, while the follow-up album cleared sales of 70,000. Brighouse appeared on *Top of the Pops* and the national press showed great interest in this new phenomenon. The band and their conductor, Derek Broadbent, hoped to use this exposure to change the public's idea of brass bands, to destroy the cloth-cap image once and for all; unfortunately, it was this very image which caught the imagination of the public and the press. Like all novelty records which do well in the pop charts, 'The Floral Dance' was soon forgotten, and although many people have heard of Brighouse and Rastrick because of it, it is with this novelty item that they, and brass bands in general, are associated and not with the more exciting activities in which they are involved.

Although these new departures might be the first things to strike the spectator, the centre of the bandsman's world was still contesting, and most especially the Belle Vue Open and the National Festival at the Albert Hall. The Belle Vue Pleasure Gardens were bought by a large public company in the mid-1970s, and Harry Mortimer took over direction of the Spring Festival and the September Championship. The winners of the Grand Shield, the top class of the Spring Festival, gain automatic entry to the Open in September, and the rest of the bands are there by invitation only; this, it is hoped, guarantees a top-quality field. In 1981, however, developers were ready to move in to demolish Belle Vue, and so the 1981 British Open was the 128th and last to be held there. At the end of the year Harry Mortimer conducted a massed band concert at the King's Hall, Belle Vue, to mark the passing of the historic venue; an emotional evening for all concerned. Since 1982 the British Open has been staged at the Free Trade Hall, Manchester, where it has continued to flourish. Under Harry Mortimer's direction the choice of test-pieces has been a mixture of old and new. John Ireland's 'Comedy Overture' (1934), was resurrected for 1984, and Percy Fletcher's 'An Epic Symphony' (1926) for 1976. New pieces have included, in 1983, 'Connotations for Brass Band' by Edward Gregson, the 1977 National test-piece, and in 1975 the Howarth 'Fireworks' already mentioned.

The National has had a more troubled recent history. When E. Vaughan Morris retired as the organizer and owner in 1971, ownership passed to the *British Bandsman*, who appointed Peter Wilson as organizing secretary. The World Championship was dropped after 1971; as an experiment it had not been terribly successful. In 1975 Robert Alexander bought the *British Bandsman* and the National Championship, and although ownership of the newspaper passed to Rosehill Instruments in 1977, Alexander kept control of the contest and its qualifying rounds. Robert Alexander's greatest contribution was the successful introduction in 1978 of the European Championship, which was held the day after the National on the Sunday. This competition played an important role in boosting continental banding, and there has always been a keen continental interest, although only British bands have won it so far. However, despite some financial backing from Bank America Finance in 1980, the National Championship nearly fell to pieces in 1981. The instrument manufacturers Boosey and Hawkes rescued the contest and set up Boosey and Hawkes Band Festivals Ltd. under the direction of Bill Martin, to supervise the European and the National. In 1983 the European Championship was held outside Britain for the first time, at Kerkrade in Holland, and became divorced from the National Festival as the latter's format changed. Traditionally the lower sections had competed at various halls around London, but Bill Martin decided to unite the entire festival under the roof of the Royal Albert Hall. Nowadays the fourth and third section finals and the Gala Concert are held on the Saturday, while the second and Championship section events have been moved to the Sunday. The National's test-pieces have been rather more adventurous than the Open's. New pieces have included 'Blitz' (1981) and 'Diversions' (1986) by Derek Bourgeois, 'Cloudcatcher Fells' (1985) by John McCabe, 'Volcano' (1979) by Robert Simpson, and 'Connotations for Brass Band' (1977) and 'Dances and Arias' (1984) by Edward Gregson.

Success in the two great championships is still the yardstick by which a band's standing is measured in the band world, and such calculations clearly show that Black Dyke Mills Band is the top band of the modern era. The results speak for themselves: since 1970 Dyke have been Open Champions in 1972, '73, '74, '76, '77, '83, '85 and '86; National Champions in 1972, '75, '76, '77, '79, '81 and '85; European Champions in 1978, '79, '82, '83, '84, '85 and '87; World Champions in 1970. Apart from this extraordinary record, Black Dyke have played an important role in the introduction of the new repertoire, have performed at the Proms, toured extensively abroad and become the first brass band to appear on compact disc, with their recording of the 1981 National test-piece, 'Blitz' by Derek Bourgeois.

No other band can match Dyke's contest record, but a number have been busy exploring new areas of activity. As we have seen, Brighouse and Rastrick's most notable success was with 'The Floral Dance', which won them much radio and television exposure. But Brighouse have also been successful in the contest arena, winning the National in 1973 and 1980, the Open in 1978 and the European Championship in 1981.

In some respects rivalry between Grimethorpe Colliery Band and Black Dyke Mills was a central talking-point of the 1970s; some felt that Grimethorpe's innovations were eclipsed by Dyke's contest record, while others thought

Dyke's attitude reactionary and Grimethorpe's important and exciting. Of course, neither view presented the full picture: Dyke performed new music, and Grimethorpe performed creditably in competition, including victory in the Open in 1984. Entertainment contests became Grimethorpe's speciality (contests, it should be noted, that Dyke refused to enter), in which they and Desford Colliery Dowty Band virtually established a monopoly.

The other Yorkshire band to perform conspicuously well has been Yorkshire Imperial Metals Band from Stourton, near Leeds. Its successes include Open titles in 1970, 1971 and 1980 and the National Championship of 1978.

Old favourites have also gained some success since 1970. Besses o' th' Barn have commioned and performed much new music, as well as winning the Open in 1982, their first major title since the Open of 1959. Williams Fairey Band (formerly Fairey Aviation Works, then Fairey Engineering Works) tasted victory for the first time since their double of 1965 when they became Open Champions in 1979 and National Champions in 1986. Wingates Temperance had achieved the double in successive years in 1906 and 1907, and had been the leading band in the years before the Second World War; but the post-war years had been somewhat fallow until their popular victory at Belle Vue in 1975.

Three other bands stand out. Cory Band from the Rhondda Valley won the National in 1974 but then went into something of a decline, as mentioned by Bram Gay in Chapter 3. But now in the 1980s they have returned to prominence with a hat-trick of National titles in 1982, 1983 and 1984, and the European title in 1980. Desford Colliery Dowty Band have perhaps been the discovery of the 1980s. They have performed extremely well in entertainment contests such as the Granada and the Rothmans, won the European Championship in 1986, and were named 'Champions of Champions' in 1982, at a one-off contest between the title-holders of the five major championships. With their musical director, Howard Snell, they have commissioned new work, as well as won much popularity for performances of their unique 'home-grown' repertoire. Stanshawe Band from Bristol have figured highly among the prizewinners of the major titles without having won either championship, but their adventurous programming under Derek Bourgeois has made the band an important and interesting force during the last ten years.

If contesting and repertoire have been healthy during the 1970s and 1980s, financially bands have often been in difficulties. Many of the traditional links with sponsoring firms, some of which also provided bandsmen with employment, have been severed. Although nineteen members of Grimethorpe Colliery Band work at the colliery, this is the exception rather than the rule and new players joining the band may not be so lucky in finding a ready-made job. None of the Black Dyke Mills Band works for John Foster and Sons any more, but the firm continues to sponsor the band because it provides good advertising and preserves an age-old relationship. Other bands have had to find new sponsors. Foden's Motor Works no longer supports the band that bears its name, which is now sponsored by Britannia Building Society. Desford Colliery was closed down some years ago, but the band has won support from elsewhere to become the Desford Colliery Dowty Band. Similarly, Wingates dropped the 'Temperance' from their name and a few months later signed a sponsorship deal with Bass breweries. Few bands have been able to survive without support – Brighouse, who made a great deal of money from 'The Floral Dance', are an exception – and it is to be hoped that firms will continue to sponsor banding because, without their assistance, many top bands could begin to fade or even disappear altogether.

Apart from these giants, most bands spend their lives in relative obscurity, often struggling even harder to make ends meet. Henry Livings's book *That the Medals and the Baton be put on view* gives the best account of how a small local band overcomes its financial difficulties. This is a world where sales of work, raffles, dances and concerts provide the basic funds for the band, supplemented by occasional support from the local education authority. Brass bands are basically uneconomic in an age in which 'uneconomic' is a dirty word, but such is the grip that this way of life has on those who participate that the bands usually muddle through, thanks to the dedicated work of the bandsmen and their supporters. The local contesting circuit is healthy – the *British Bandsman* reports on over a hundred contests a year, and those are only the ones that they receive information about. Indeed, the magazine is full of details of local banding activities, which would suggest that bands are persevering and many are flourishing despite the odds which are stacked against them. The Whit Friday Quickstep Contests in Saddleworth can attract crowds of up to 40,000, who come to watch the small bands like Dobcross tackle the might of Black Dyke and Brighouse and Rastrick in a series of village contests. Such events lie at the heart of the movement and are a tribute to the people who organize and participate in them – their enthusiasm keeps the movement alive just as much as the bands and bandsmen who triumph on the stages of the Royal Albert Hall or the Free Trade Hall every year.

Possibly the most important area of banding today is the explosion in the number of youth bands that has occurred in the last twenty years. The availability of brass teaching in schools has done much to promote this. At the beginning of the nineteenth century it was thought that brass instruments were suitable for the working man because they were hardy and a player could produce a decent noise on one relatively quickly, and the same reasons hold good for a girl or boy wanting to become involved in music at school. The provision of instruments has become more of a problem as lack of money has begun to affect all areas of the education system, with the result that pupils have to learn whichever type of instrument is available, much as those learning a hundred years ago had to do. But when a little hard work produces such exciting rewards quite quickly, many young players want to become involved with brass, and from then on are often hooked for life. Many towns and counties now have their own youth bands which are doing exciting things, often including musical trips to the Continent to help spread the word. What is especially encouraging about this expansion is that it is taking place in many areas which have had no banding tradition, and is therefore both introducing a new audience to bands and bringing in new blood to participate actively, which must bode well for the long-term future of the movement. Money is always the problem, and it is a pity that there is not more support from the bigger bands, for whom investment in youth would almost certainly pay off – very few of the major bands contribute to fund-raising efforts for the National Youth Brass Band, despite the fact that many of the young players will move on to play in these very bands and therefore help to keep them at the top. The wider musical world also has a part to play – many of our best orchestral brass players come from a banding background; James Watson of Covent Garden and Maurice Murphy of the London Symphony Orchestra are just two. Anyone interested in the arts should want to support a system which is producing people who will help to ensure the future prosperity of our cultural life.

Despite all this activity, much of it exciting and important, many feel that banding remains weak and vulnerable. Much of this concern is about the lack of any central organization in the band movement. But bands have always rebelled against any such idea, and it is true that the regional associations have continued to organize themselves efficiently. While a spirit of independence is generally a good thing, however, the lack of co-operation and central leadership can have debilitating effects. When the National was in danger of collapse in 1981 the bands found themselves powerless to do anything about it, and it was up to Boosey and Hawkes to rescue the contest. For such a fiercely independent movement it seems strange that brass banding is so reliant upon the goodwill and sponsorship of others. There is no reason why the bands themselves should not appoint an organization to run their activities on their behalf; indeed, it would seem to be in their interest to do so. It is also in their interest to look after one another and their future – the lack of support for an institution like the National Youth Brass Band is scandalous, and the top bands in particular are in danger of cutting their own throats if they don't begin to take their responsibilities seriously. Many people have stressed how important is the need for a central association, and bandsmen and their supporters must begin to debate this question soon if they are to continue to grow and progress in the 1990s.

8

Song

A Composer: Derek Bourgeois

DEREK BOURGEOIS IS one of Britain's best-known composers. While a lecturer on music at the University of Bristol, he was introduced to brass bands and became Musical Director of the Stanshawe Band in 1980. His compositions for band are many and varied; they include two concertos, and the National Championship test-pieces 'Blitz' (1981) and 'Diversions' (1986). He is now Musical Director of the National Youth Orchestra. Patrick Howarth talked to him in July 1987, during the orchestra's summer course at Cranleigh School, Surrey, of which Derek Bourgeois himself is an old boy.

PATRICK HOWARTH: *Do you come from a brass band background?*

DEREK BOURGEOIS: Not at all; no real musical background at all, really.

At the end of the war my parents bought a small piano, sat me at it and I started to smash away at it. They realised that since I was showing an interest in the sounds it made, it would be a good idea to get me some piano lessons – so when I was six they sent me down to a local piano teacher, who was actually a very bad teacher. I kept the lessons going when I went to school, but it wasn't until about the age of thirteen that I began to show any serious interest in writing music.

125

PATRICK HOWARTH: *Did you just suddenly start to jot things down?*

DEREK BOURGEOIS: No, I had jotted things down right from the beginning, because at the same time as getting the piano and starting to learn notation, one of the first pieces I had was in a little book which contained some Mozart piano pieces written when he was five – well, I was six already and thought I must be missing out on this. My parents bought me a manuscript book which I filled up with totally indecipherable hieroglyphics. So I always jotted things down, but it wasn't until I was thirteen that I had any formal training in what notated music really ought to be.

PATRICK HOWARTH: *Was that at school?*

DEREK BOURGEOIS: Yes; which, strangely enough, was this school here, Cranleigh. I had my first harmony and counterpoint lessons here, and began to find out if what I had been doing up to that time had been right or wrong – it was mainly wrong, in fact.

PATRICK HOWARTH: *What were you writing for in those days?*

DEREK BOURGEOIS: I started off writing for piano, but then had delusions of grandeur and began scoring for a large orchestra. But I was put off that and told that one really should start from the beginning with little pieces and move on from there. Then a master at the school wrote some music for the school play, scored for a small ensemble including tuba. About three days before the play was going to start the tuba player fell ill, so they gave me a tuba, saying 'Here, learn this.' I managed somehow to get through the production, and within a year was in the National Youth Orchestra. That's where I really began to learn about orchestration and brass playing properly – it was all rather sudden and late.

PATRICK HOWARTH: *Where did you go after school?*

DEREK BOURGEOIS: Cambridge and then the Royal College of Music.

PATRICK HOWARTH: *And still no involvement with brass bands?*

DEREK BOURGEOIS: No, none whatsoever. It was your father who suggested I do something for brass band. He sent me a copy of the record 'Pop Goes the Posthorn' and a list of instruments and their ranges, and said, 'If you produce something, I'll try it out with Grimethorpe.' I'd never done anything like that before and, quite honestly, up until then had never encountered a brass band, apart from the record he gave me.

PATRICK HOWARTH: *So when you began to write you were totally unaware of the brass band world?*

DEREK BOURGEOIS: Yes, totally unaware. The first Concerto for Brass Band was the direct result of those circumstances, but of course in no time at all I found myself knowing a lot about brass bands. It was absolutely instantaneous – I was thirty-three and until then completely ignorant of them.

PATRICK HOWARTH: *You had been writing a great deal before, of course.*

DEREK BOURGEOIS: Oh, yes, I had written quite a lot of brass music before this time, but it had always been for orchestral brass.

PATRICK HOWARTH: *Is that how you met my father?*

DEREK BOURGEOIS: Yes, when a quintet I had actually

written for Bram Gay when he was in the
Hallé, but which he had never played, was
premièred by the Philip Jones ensemble in
1968. Ironically enough, that recital was
here at Cranleigh, too. They claimed the
piece was unplayable, something which
seems to follow me around whatever I do!

PATRICK HOWARTH: *Apart from composition, you have also
been involved in the performing side of the
band world.*

DEREK BOURGEOIS: Yes. I had conducting lessons with Sir
Adrian Boult when I was at the Royal
College, which were actually very valuable
because he was very good at conveying the
principles of conducting and the dos and
don'ts. I think it's very important for a
composer to be able to see his way through
his own music, if need be.

PATRICK HOWARTH: *Do you often conduct your own music?*

DEREK BOURGEOIS: I wouldn't say often, but not infrequent-
ly. I quite enjoy conducting my own music,
because I feel I know it as well as anybody
could. Although I do enjoy hearing different interpretations of pieces, I sometimes
get rather irritated at total misunderstand-
ing of what's written on the page.

PATRICK HOWARTH: *When did you start conducting bands?*

DEREK BOURGEOIS: The very first time I ever waved at a
brass band was during a rehearsal of the
concerto we've talked about, when
Grimethorpe took it down to the Queen
Elizabeth Hall in London and your father
said, 'Just take over for a few minutes,
while I go to the back to listen to the
balance.' The next time was your father's
fault, too. I'd written a second concerto,
which was commissioned for the Norwich

Triennial Festival in 1976. I arrived at St Andrew's Hall in the morning just to listen to the rehearsal, and your Dad said that he thought it would be a nice idea if I conducted it. It's all very well having written a piece, but that particular concerto is quite complicated to conduct, and I'd done no homework on where the actual stick goes when I suddenly found myself thrust in front of this band, having to learn how to conduct it almost immediately – quite a terrifying experience.

PATRICK HOWARTH: *What were your first impressions of Grimethorpe, since it was the first band you had really ever listened to?*

DEREK BOURGEOIS: It was the first brass band that I'd ever encountered. I was just knocked over at their ability to get around the notes, the incredible tightness of the ensemble, and the extraordinary incongruity between what they played and the human beings they were. It was almost a culture shock to find that people of such delightful earthiness could suddenly pick up all these instruments and away they'd go – it was amazing, and spurred a tremendous interest in me, and within no time at all I'd worked out what the brass band movement was all about. Perhaps the unfortunate thing was my not realising at first that not all brass bands were as good as that. I'd started, as it were, at the top of the tree and had to work down it.

The next encounter was with the then Stanshawe Band in Bristol[1].

PATRICK HOWARTH: *They would have been your local band, I suppose?*

1 Now Sun Life Band

DEREK BOURGEOIS: That's right, because I was teaching at the University at that time. We were holding a little festival there, and we wanted as wide a variety of media as possible, so I approached them about doing a concert for us. They performed my second concerto at that concert and I got to know them a bit, but it wasn't until about two years later that they approached me about becoming their professional conductor. I stayed there for about three or four years, and in that time got to know all the repertoire, and the ways of brass bands; it was a very valuable time. It also did another thing: it actually taught me as a composer that there was a breed of musician with whom you could not get away with anything. If they liked something, then they liked it, even if they didn't know why, but if they didn't like something, they didn't half let you know! By and large their taste was good; they didn't know why they liked or disliked a piece – it wasn't a question of how modern it sounded or how popular it was – but they did have some sort of corporate taste, which was extremely down-to-earth and extremely reliable. It taught me that intellectual posturing was actually no good at all if it didn't have some spark in it which could appeal to this highly developed, but untrained, sense of taste.

PATRICK HOWARTH: *Did you learn much as a conductor as well as a composer?*

DEREK BOURGEOIS: An enormous amount. For instance, when you're preparing a piece for a brass band contest, you get an opportunity you never have with an orchestra – apart maybe from a highly trained youth orchestra – to get all the details absolutely correct. There is time to pull a piece to bits and put it right. The very first piece Stanshawe ever gave me for a contest was the Berlioz overture *Benvenuto Cellini,* and we had forty-four hours of rehearsal for that one piece. I had to learn how to use forty-four hours of rehearsal time and still find something relevant to say at the end of it. It was certainly a very hard but very exciting lesson.

PATRICK HOWARTH: *What did you make of the major competitions when you first encountered them?*

DEREK BOURGEOIS: I conducted Stanshawe at the Open, but the first time I had the chance to conduct them at the National, Boosey and Hawkes wouldn't let me because it was my own test-piece.

PATRICK HOWARTH: *Was that 'Blitz'?*

DEREK BOURGEOIS: Yes. They seemed to think that the composer would have some unfair advantage over all the others. I've never quite understood that way of thinking – the notes are there for everybody.

PATRICK HOWARTH: *Did you adjudicate?*

DEREK BOURGEOIS: No. They wouldn't let me do that, either, so I just had to sit there and listen to it.

PATRICK HOWARTH: *So what were your impressions of this incredible event?*

DEREK BOURGEOIS: My very first reaction to the first contest that I went to was: how can the audience stand listening to the same piece of music over and over again? It was a sort of mentality I hadn't got used to at that point. My whole idea of concert programming is to get as much variety as possible – if not total variety of pieces, at least some sort of interesting pattern of events going on so that you progress from one piece to another in a logical and varied way. The thought of having groups sitting there playing the same piece over and over again seemed utterly alien to me; indeed, I'm not sure if it still isn't.

PATRICK HOWARTH: *Can you think of anything like it?*

DEREK BOURGEOIS: No, I can't. At least if you're listening to the Leeds Piano Competition you hear six different concerti. Similarly with the Young Musician of the Year, the pieces are not the same. All other competitive musical sports provide a varied diet, and from that point of view I feel that the entertainment contests are much more interesting to be part of.

PATRICK HOWARTH: *Have you conducted at entertainment contests?*

DEREK BOURGEOIS: I've done the Granada several times. We never won it, although we came quite high up a number of times. I made the mistake the first time of being a bit too highbrow; I soon learnt after that the right mixture of the serious and the light-hearted. One of the things you learn by being associated with brass bands is that you can be brought down to earth with a bump – if you have your head in the clouds it won't stay there long. I found that very valuable, having contact with very gifted but unknowledgeable musical people. When you're surrounded by very know-ledgeable musical people there's a certain degree of trying to outwit the musical expert that goes on and you become somewhat esoteric. You can't be esoteric in front of a brass band without being laughed out of court.

PATRICK HOWARTH: *Do you think that has influenced your writing a great deal?*

DEREK BOURGEOIS: It certainly changed it very dramatically at that point.

PATRICK HOWARTH: *Has it continued to change it?*

DEREK BOURGEOIS: Yes, it has, even though I no longer have a great deal to do with brass bands directly. Having taken on the National Youth Orchestra, that's a pretty full-time job. The lesson I learnt then about musical taste, what the average musician thinks, certainly had some influence, but there are lots of other influences as well.

I still find the whole of the musical composing scene a very great dilemma. I think that music did reach a very critical point in the middle of the 1960s, which was exactly when I was starting out as a composer, and I found the dilemma then almost intolerable. I found that I really couldn't keep up with the musical Joneses at that time and with all the experimentation that was going on; I could find no point of contact with an awful lot of it, although I strove to find that point of contact. There has been a very great change since then but, like any critical point in musical history, it has gone off at umpteen tangents; and I don't think we have reached a point yet where any of those tangents have met to form any real kind of mainstream. It may be just round the corner, I don't know.

But what does strike me very forcibly is that this thing that we now call classical music seems to have drifted far away from being the mainstream of musical consciousness in the general world at large. For instance, in the seventeenth and eighteenth centuries the Church was the biggest patron, and then the Court, and the whole concept at that time was one of instant disposable music. Bach wouldn't have written all those cantatas, and Telemann even more, if they had expected any of them to go down in history as musical masterpieces. The idea was that they wrote one for one Sunday, chucked it away and got on with the next one – likewise the Haydn symphonies. The exact equivalent today seems to me to be the music written for the media, for television and films. That is instant and disposable – you write your episode of *Kojak* one week, and write the next one the next week. That is an extreme example, perhaps, but it does seem to me to be the modern equivalent, while the highbrow concert music is now very much a minority interest, no longer the main flow of musical composition throughout the world.

PATRICK HOWARTH: *When you say that highbrow classical music is no longer the mainstream, do you feel that the music must become more of the mainstream or that the mainstream must move to include that music?*

DEREK BOURGEOIS: It may well be that classical concerts as we know them are no longer any sort of mainstream, either. Let's face it, all our concert-going activities are devoted to maintaining what can only be described as museum culture. The vast majority of works being played at concerts, in this country in particular, are still part of the same repertoire as fifty years ago. In percentage terms the amount of new music, or music of the recent past, being played is very small. There is no general willingness on the part of players, managers and the general public to bring the repertoire up to date. Now, if you go back a hundred years you will find that the majority of the repertoire was contemporary – at a concert in 1887 you would be listening to new works by Dvořák, Tchaikovsky and Strauss. People were also very interested – there were great wars of words between supporters of Brahms and supporters of Wagner; it was very healthy. You don't get the same interest in the general music-going public now as you once did. Here's an example. Vaughan Williams's Sixth Symphony, first performed in 1948, had one hundred performances in its first two years; ten years ago, in 1977, Tippett's Fourth Symphony had two. That's symptomatic – even something that is acknowledged as a masterpiece only gets performed a perfunctory number of times.

PATRICK HOWARTH: *Some people feel that similar problems are facing brass bands, but how do you get your audience back?*

DEREK BOURGEOIS: How much do you think they've lost? They still have vast audiences for brass bands compared with those for orchestras. Though it may not be what it used to. The availability of very high-quality home reproduction is bound to have an effect on all activities which require people to go out and get somewhere. I think this applies to all walks of life, not just music. It can be said of sport, and will soon probably be said of shopping, now you have these phone computers where you order what you want and it gets delivered to your doorstep. Mechanization seems to be leading to inactivity on a wide scale. But the introduction of the compact disc, and the price of records having fallen in real terms about ten times since the 1950s, means that people can enjoy music in their own homes without having to go out and pay for it. Concerts are cheap in relative terms, but getting there isn't – if you take your family out to a concert you have the bother of a meal and all the rest of it; it's becoming an expensive night out. But how much have brass band audiences dropped, do you think?

PATRICK HOWARTH: *The traditionalism that has built up in the brass band world has created a very loyal hardcore audience, I suppose.*

DEREK BOURGEOIS: Part of the brass band world's problem, I think – and this applies to all the other media as well – is that the very traditionalism it seeks to retain will eventually alienate the other people. Without change it will become less and less relevant to each succeeding generation. The brass band world is the most unchangeable I've ever encountered; even the most modest of changes is resisted fiercely. The thought of changing instrumentation in any way whatsoever, the idea of introducing a trumpet into a band, is regarded as a heinous crime. The same applies to all its other traditions.

PATRICK HOWARTH: *How quickly did you become aware of this?*

DEREK BOURGEOIS: Immensely quickly, because when I encountered the movement as a whole it was the thing that stood out more than anything else. Here was something that was almost a fossil – a living fossil, and a very enjoyable fossil – but unchangeable. I think that anything that is not prepared to change, not necessarily drastically, but that won't move with the times – and the brass band world won't do that, it won't change its format in any way – is bound to become irrelevant eventually.

PATRICK HOWARTH: *Irrelevant to whom?*

DEREK BOURGEOIS: To people who take part in it.

PATRICK HOWARTH: *Surely it will always be relevant to those people?*

DEREK BOURGEOIS: Yes, but they are getting older and older, and unless it changes it will die with them.

I don't believe in revolution but I do believe in evolution. The brass band movement has tried to stop evolution at a certain point in its history, and is very resistant to moving on from there. Curiously enough, it is much more prepared to be evolutionary in its repertoire than in its constituents – which is very strange. Contesting keeps the standards up, but also keeps any change in instrumentation, for example, out of line.

PATRICK HOWARTH: *There does seem to have been a minor revolution when percussion was admitted to contests in 1972.*

DEREK BOURGEOIS: Yes, that was a great revolution, although percussion parts had always been in the score – they just weren't allowed to be used in contests. I remember one thing we were doing at Stanshawe, which wasn't for a contest but, rather, for a concert. I had found out that some of the cornet players had trumpets, and I wanted to use three trumpets in among the cornets in the arrangement I had done, in order to try for some colours. They thought about it but said no, because it was too much of a change, even though some of them owned and played trumpets. They were frightened of making an exhibition which would set the whole band world against them.

PATRICK HOWARTH: *Ken Hirst said something very similar – that the players liked playing modern works but were embarrassed at springing something unexpected on their audience.*

DEREK BOURGEOIS: Yes, that's right. They are terrified of being embarrassed in front of their audience. What I'm trying to say is that the audience will carry on diminishing while the traditions only appeal to an ever-ageing audience. Unless you can introduce new elements into the system which will appeal to younger people, then you can't win through. It will take a long time to die out – any musical culture will take a long time to die out – but it will unless there is evolution. You only have to look at any of the great civilizations which have died out to discover that a decadence sets in and, once it has become established, that is the beginning of the end. And I do detect in much of our musical life in general, not just brass bands, that decadence is all around us.

We may be missing the point that the culture we are so interested in, the world of brass bands or orchestral music, is being superseded by something else. The huge electronic revolution – which really is a revolution – the amazing jump forward in the discoveries in microcircuitry, the new chips coming in, will make the ones we have at the moment look incredibly old-fashioned in a couple of years. What is possible in musical synthesis is becoming more and more sophisticated. We haven't seen anything yet, I'm sure of that.

PATRICK HOWARTH: *Do you think that home music-making using electronics could be the musical pastime of the future?*

DEREK BOURGEOIS: It already is. Look at what the synthesizer can do now compared with ten years ago, and these are only keyboard synthesizers; at least, the commercial ones are. But they are doing vast amounts of experimentation on things involving bowed, plucked and blown instruments, as well as all the sampling that's going on, and it's getting cheaper and cheaper. The pop world has virtually been taken over by these instruments already, acoustic instruments are virtually dead, and all that has happened in fifteen years, if that. It will take longer to permeate the bastions of brass bands and the orchestral world, but they can't ignore it completely, and where it will all lead no one can tell.

PATRICK HOWARTH: *Can we move on to talk about test-pieces now, for example 'Blitz'. What are the inherent difficulties in writing a test-piece for the National?*

DEREK BOURGEOIS: The one thing that's worth saying about 'Blitz' is that it was written just before I took on a brass band as the professional conductor, and if I had written it six months later it would have been very different. I wrote it before I really knew what was difficult and what was not. The ideal test-piece is one which, first of all, keeps the audience happy throughout its umpteen performances – in other words, the audience will get more each time they hear it, so that by the end of the contest they will have really got to grips with the piece. The trouble is that that applies to the adjudicators too, which is why with a new test-piece it is very difficult for the early bands to make an impression, because the judges are learning the work as well. I don't care what you say about how much they have the score in advance; they don't really know the piece until they have heard it half a dozen times.

It must also be a piece which tests all the different aspects of the band, its ensemble, its nerve, its ability to play quietly, its ability to play expressively. Obviously it must test the individual ability of each section, which I don't think many test-pieces do. Above all, it must be a good piece of music as well. So the criteria for writing a good test-piece are very demanding. I'm not sure that I have written the ideal test-piece yet, because my first one, 'Blitz', I wrote before I knew much about brass bands, and the one they used in 1986 was never intended to be a test-piece – although, strangely enough, it proved to be quite challenging. But if anybody ever asks me to write a championship test-piece again, I think it would be a very different animal from the ones that I have done already.

There are also all sorts of questions of style and fashion with brass bands. I personally do not like the old-fashioned wide vibrato style, which some people still write to the *British Bandsman* about, bemoaning its disappearance. I do much prefer a cleaner sound; obviously a little bit of colour in expressive passages is fine, but not the out-of-control, old-fashioned vibrato.

PATRICK HOWARTH: *Would you like to write more?*

DEREK BOURGEOIS: I like writing music for brass band very much. Curiously enough, I do have an ambition, which may not seem a very positive one. I should like to bc asked to write test-pieces for a lot of the lower sections. I should like to get clear in my own mind the exact differences between the Championship and the second section, and the third, fourth and Youth sections.

PATRICK HOWARTH: *Have you done any work for the lower sections?*

DEREK BOURGEOIS: I have done a third section test-piece, which I actually wrote for the fourth section, but Boosey's thought it was right for the higher section, mistakenly in my opinion.

PATRICK HOWARTH: *In some ways writing for the lower sections must be even more of a challenge than writing for the top bands in the Championship section.*

DEREK BOURGEOIS: Oh, it is. To make the music interesting for the lower sections is a great challenge. As I said at the beginning, I do regret having started at the top and worked down; it's the wrong way to do it and is even slightly harder that way round.

I don't have any grandiose ambitions, as it were, but I do have one sadness. I tried to do with Stanshawe what your father did with Grimethorpe; that is, to make them a serious band which played at serious music festivals instead of just doing their end-of-pier concerts, which they loved. I wanted to take some serious repertoire and be invited abroad to foreign music festivals and to festivals in this country, such as Cheltenham or Bath. To get a reputation for doing that sort of thing is a great challenge, and although the band enjoyed the challenge they couldn't quite reconcile in their minds the dropping of the other image while this was going on. It became too much of a pull for them, and in the end they wouldn't go along with it. I was very sad about that, because I think they could have done it, and it would have been an evolutionary step. The gulf between the brass band audience and the symphony orchestra audience needn't exist, and I was hoping to bridge that gulf. I did start to do it, but found almost insurmountable opposition eventually. The band couldn't make up its mind and got cold feet, even though we had made one or two interesting sallies into that world.

PATRICK HOWARTH: *Had you done much commissioning for the band?*

DEREK BOURGEOIS: Yes. I commissioned a number of pieces and tried to perform as many new pieces as possible. I do think that the life-blood of any musical organization is its ability to play contemporary repertoire. You cannot expect the masterpieces of today to emerge unless works have had enough exposure for people to realize whether a work is a masterpiece or not. The reason why the great masterpieces of the last century and the beginning of this century have become established is that they had enough exposure for people to realize that they had this stature. Contemporary music today is only performed once or twice, and it can't prove that it has enough stature without exposure.

PATRICK HOWARTH: *When you were at Bristol University as a lecturer in music, was there any brass band involvement in your courses? Is there a place for the brass band in higher education?*

DEREK BOURGEOIS: There is a place now, of course: Salford have had their degree course ratified, which I think is fascinating. I know there are a lot of sceptics, but I say good luck to them. The only slight worry I have is whether they will teach the subject at a high enough level to people who are of a high enough standard to make use of it. But the academic content of the course is in theory quite high enough to warrant a degree at the end of it.

PATRICK HOWARTH: *Do you think brass banding could become part of a more general music degree?*

DEREK BOURGEOIS: You'll never get a brass band at a university, because you won't get enough people coming to a university to be able to form a brass band, in the way that you can usually form an orchestra, because you need such specific requirements. Certainly at Bristol we did introduce questions about the brass band repertoire into some of the more general historical papers, and nobody demurred against that at all. We did have one or two students who were brass band players, most notably Steven Mead, who is with Desford now. He gave a euphonium recital as part of his final degree, and did it very well, too. The performing option, apart from the recital, was history and repertoire of the instrument, which included general brass band repertoire, because there was not enough euphonium repertoire to fill up a paper.

PATRICK HOWARTH: *What sort of questions did you include in the paper?*

DEREK BOURGEOIS: An analytical review of trends – in fact, very much the same questions as you have been asking me. We asked searching questions about history, development and the future, such as 'Has the brass band got stuck?' There was a wide variety, including questions about the origins of the instruments and specific periods and their repertoire. He also had to do some scoring for band as well. At Bristol we tried to tailor-make the papers around what each student was interested in, while expecting a high standard of academic endeavour to be shown within each area of interest. Just because Steven was a very good euphonium player, it didn't mean that he would get a good degree without doing the necessary background work for his subject.

PATRICK HOWARTH: *Have you been up to Salford?*

DEREK BOURGEOIS: Yes, last May. I gave them a lecture on brass and wind band scoring. I saw all around the place, and it seems a very worthwhile experiment, but we must wait and see if it succeeds. If it doesn't succeed, I think it may be because it failed to attract a high enough calibre of student. I think the building they are in may cause problems; it is not exactly the most pleasant place to work in. If they get enough capital put into it, that will help. I hope it succeeds.

Brighouse and Rastrick Band in 1885   *Dennis Hussey*

THE PLAYER: Bram Gay   *Margaret Gay*

THE ADMINISTRATOR: Ken Hirst on tour i[n]
Australia

The Conductor: Major Peter Parkes

The Composer: Derek Bourgeois

National Youth Brass Band, Harrogate 1987

PATRICK HOWARTH: *Are you working on anything for band at the moment?*

DEREK BOURGEOIS: Yes, I am working on a little piece. Strangely enough, it's for Salford; they want a sort of pot-boiler to use as an encore piece. They are the hardest to write, actually – it's much more difficult to write something catchy and attractive than to do something important. You can hide behind a major work's importance to some extent, whereas an encore must have something immediately accessible about it which keeps bringing people back to it, which is the hardest thing to find of the lot.

The next piece on the list is one for a ten-piece brass group, of about fifteen minutes' duration, which I suppose may eventually find its way into a transcription for brass band. Of all the brass band pieces I've ever written, most are transcriptions from other works. I'm quite a believer in transcriptions, because it is perfectly possible to change a piece from one medium to another if you take enough care over it; I think it's quite a useful way of getting one piece into various different media.

PATRICK HOWARTH: *Do you do much arranging?*

DEREK BOURGEOIS: I used to do an awful lot when I was with Stanshawe. I did Dukas' *Sorcerer's Apprentice* and lots more minor pieces. I used to arrange a lot of pieces simply for Stanshawe to take around to concerts. I tried to get permission to do the entire *Rite of Spring,* which I thought would really knock them for six, but the Stravinsky estate wouldn't allow it. I was rather sore about that, because Ray Farr [conductor of Grimethorpe Colliery Band 1980-85]

went ahead and did the *Firebird* Suite
without permission, and once he had done
it the estate obligingly said OK. I went
through the proper channels and they said
no. It's a pity, because I do think it would
work – the writing in that piece is absolutely tailor-made for a brass band transcription because the string writing is not
terribly important in it, apart from the
very opening passage, of course. The
writing for the wind and brass is very
monolithic and would have suited brass
band perfectly.

PATRICK HOWARTH: *You are now artistic director of the
National Youth Orchestra; is there any
connection between the orchestra and the
National Youth Brass Band?*

DEREK BOURGEOIS: We made a connection during the last
course. We did Walton's *Belshazzar's
Feast,* for which we had the National
Youth Choir, the National Youth Brass
Band and the National Youth Orchestra
all together – it must have been the largest
gathering of young musicians ever. The
brass band and choir both had pieces of
their own in the programme as well. It was
a very exciting occasion.

PATRICK HOWARTH: *Do any of the brass players in the
orchestra play in bands?*

DEREK BOURGEOIS: Quite a lot of them. Curiously, the
players who come into this orchestra from
their brass bands seem to have no trouble
switching from the cornet to the trumpet.
I've never fully understood why so many
brass bandsmen think that trumpet playing
will ruin their cornet playing.

PATRICK HOWARTH: *Do you have a favourite out of your
brass band pieces?*

DEREK BOURGEOIS: It's usually the one I've just written. Perhaps the Second Concerto was the most ambitious and serious, and it was one of the few that was really designed for band and has never been thought of as anything else.

PATRICK HOWARTH: *Do you have one memory of bands which stands out more than any of the others?*

DEREK BOURGEOIS: There were several funny incidents with Stanshawe. I had done an arrangement of 'Tico-Tico',[1] which we took down to a concert in Yeovil. In order to liven up the middle bit I had prescribed some bomb tanks, which we had tried out at the Granada unsuccessfully because, for some reason, the fuses hadn't gone off. We had all these fuses and bomb tanks left over which we wanted to use up before returning the equipment to where we'd hired it from. So at Yeovil we let the whole lot off in one go, and all the plaster fell off the ceiling on to the band. It was the most frightful noise – half the audience walked out in umbrage, thinking they were under attack.

1 A popular Latin-American number

9

Selection

Elgar Howarth on the Modern Repertoire

MUCH DESIRED BY the few, much feared by many, the new repertoire, the major change, happened suddenly in the 1970s. Now, in the late 1980s, it is not entirely clear where its direction has led; certainly not to the catastrophe forecast by the fearful, who foresaw the end of banding, the final departure of audiences, the falling of the house, the trembling of the ether; but neither to the emancipated world desired by the few, the golden era of bands in every Prom series, composers galore at every band rehearsal, forsaking the string quartet in favour of six and twenty bandsmen complete with whirling xylophones and rattling maracas, sending the old faithful guard into apoplexies of outrage.

When bands and their followers spoke of change, it was usually in the vaguest possible terms. Some felt that the 'image' was wrong, but since it was an image that had such a low profile for the general musical public that it was almost unnoticed, there should have been recognition that something particular needed changing, rather than a general woolly concept of bands becoming 'different'. Some thought that altering competition rules – open adjudication, for instance – would effect change, not realizing that such inward-looking preoccupation was exactly what was wrong; most in the movement were too close to the play to see the ball. Others, more discerning but still wide of the mark, wanted to experiment with the instrumentation of bands, uniform for years, to make for equality in contests. Others naturally wanted no change at all. The repertoire – the music played – seemed to most to be the last consideration, but when change came it was of course a new repertoire with a new emphasis which caused it.

Three factors conspired to pull bands finally, and extremely belatedly, into the mainstream of twentieth-century

148

music-making, with the result that the 1970s became the most exciting time for them since the 1930s. One was the further development of the commissioned test-piece by new composers with fresh ideas, all of them basically conservative in musical language but several steps on in terms of the status quo; a second was the invention by Bram Gay of a new type of contest (the entertainment contest), which was sponsored and televised by Granada Television; and, thirdly, there was a realization by a tiny minority that there were composers eager to write for bands, away from the contest situation, music which really reflected the current state of composition in the wider world – and that there was an audience for it.

The contest world took a considerable step in a different musical direction when, in 1971, the National commissioned Robert Simpson to write 'Energy' as the test-piece for the finals of the so-called and only briefly sustained World Championship. Simpson, a composer of conservative vocabulary, has nevertheless an extremely complex musical mind. He understood the medium, too, since as a young man he had played the flugel horn in a Salvation Army band. His piece was an essay in the control of small motifs, or cells as they are known, throughout a work where the tempo was gradually quickening. It lacked the kind of melodic comfort to which bands are accustomed and it must have frustrated one or two conductors, unable to make the normal kind of contest-winning gestures – over-grandiose allargandi or super-heated crescendi. It was a brave choice, influenced no doubt by Geoffrey Brand, who was at that time effectively in control of the National and who had ambitions to re-establish a more serious repertoire. It was not popular with many bands or audiences and has been little played since, though it was chosen as the test-piece for the Open in 1980. Its general neglect, however, is a pity, since it is a work of real substance which now has a companion-piece in 'Volcano', also commissioned by the National several years later, in 1979.[1]

1 In any case the old prejudices die hard and band audiences are still reluctant to accept test-pieces into the concert repertoire, a kind of musical apartheid which fully justifies the BBC's policy of insisting on original music in their only regular serious band spot *(Bandstand, Radio 2)*.

The years immediately following 'Energy' saw the National withdraw into conservatism, frightened perhaps by the reaction to Simpson's 'shocker', though Malcolm Arnold wrote a pleasing 'Fantasy' for the finals in 1974.

The Open, now owned and organized by Harry Mortimer, was also conscious of a need for novelty, at least. In 1975 Mortimer asked my opinion of competition pieces in general. I replied that I found many of them lacking in interest and exposure for some sections of the band. He invited me to write a test-piece reflecting my criticism, and I presented 'Fireworks' for the championships of that year.

A curious anomaly of banding had been modified only a couple of years before. Traditionally, percussion players were never allowed to perform in a contest, since it was feared that 'the drums' would cover up faults of brass playing. Even though composers wrote (often rather rudimentary) parts for, say, drums and cymbals, and even though 'the drummer' was a regular and indispensable member of the band, they were treated as pariahs, excluded from the great events of the calendar – the contests. Now, suddenly, after a lot of worried speculation, they were allowed in, two per band. I decided to give them plenty to do with a great variety of instruments, some of which were new to most bands. I was clear about my objectives: I wanted to stimulate an interest in bands by good young percussionists, whose talents were badly needed.

It created a bit of a furore. Band secretaries objected to buying some of the instruments, though they could always somehow find funds for a new tuba, a bass trombone or a 'walking out' uniform. Band fans objected to this amount of percussion on the principle that the very nature of brass bands was being threatened. Band conductors objected to the plethora of time changes – 7/8, 5/8, 2/4 and so on – with which the piece abounded. Several of them wrote to or telephoned Mortimer trying to get the work stopped, to no avail; to their complaints that it was mathematical rubbish Mortimer replied by asking innocently: 'Are you telling me you can't conduct it?' The complaints quickly stopped; all the bands managed the piece, some brilliantly (including one of the worst complainers), others less well – situation normal. Very few, in the event, were outraged by the music, which was conservative in style, being modelled on Britten's 'Young Person's Guide to the Orchestra'.

The percussion argument was further resolved a couple of years later, in 1977, by Edward Gregson in his 'Connotations for Brass Band' for the National final; the percussion was featured in such an artistic way that there was no outcry. The piece, like many from the same composer, has become a great favourite with bands and is played fairly often, in contests and even in concert. Gregson has been, and remains, an important composer for bands; his style combines rhythmic vitality, lyricism and a progressive type of tonal harmony to which the traditionalists and forward thinkers alike have responded. He has also been an important influence during the 1980s as a member of the panel which chooses test-pieces for the National, now organized by Boosey and Hawkes.

Since 1975 the Open has rested on its laurels, using already existing scores of both original music and orchestral transcriptions, no doubt to the satisfaction of its audience, which likes what it knows. The one exception was in 1986, when Howard Blake's 'Fusions' was used. There is, in fact, a good musical argument for the Open serving as an antidote to the more progressive thinking of the National. It is widely felt among the more senior members of the band fraternity that bands, through coping with the generally tougher, rhythmically demanding new scores, are losing or sacrificing some of their traditional qualities, lyricism above all. It is felt that the ability to play a melody is becoming a lost art; this even though they may only play one of these new pieces a year. It is perhaps appropriate that Harry Mortimer, once the prince of lyrical cornet playing, should in his great seniority seek to redress the balance by choosing, by and large, repertoire which emphasises old virtues.

The National has also been aware of this problem and, with one or two notable exceptions, the choice made for the area contests has been 'softer' than for the London finals. It doesn't do, either, to be too hard-nosed with local audiences. One particular work which found disfavour with bands and audiences alike in this respect was John McCabe's

'Images' of 1983. McCabe's music can be dour, and this piece seemed especially impenetrable to many whose first priority, understandably enough, is a 'good day's banding'.

The National in London, however, has been both bold and successful in ordering a list of works whose musical content might have enraged and perplexed an audience twenty years ago, but which now finds the ground well prepared for such developments. Since 'Connotations' in 1977, arrangements have only been used twice, and one of these, in 1978, was a very worthwhile suite from *Checkmate,* the popular ballet score of Arthur Bliss. Simpson's 'Volcano' followed in 1979, and in 1981 Derek Bourgeois presented his 'Blitz'. We shall examine Bourgeois' contribution to the band repertoire later; suffice it to say here that the piece proved to be a great success and is often chosen by bands in 'own-choice' contests – the half-leg of the European Championship, for instance.

Wilfred Heaton's 'Contest Music' was again a serious work which proved a great test technically and musically to all in 1982. Heaton, from a Salvation Army background, understands the medium superbly, though is curiously reluctant to commit himself to it. He suffered a great disappointment in 1972 when, having completed this piece, he saw it withdrawn by a panel made timid by the often sparse nature of the score and by the reaction to 'Energy' the year before. A decade later 'Contest Music' held no terrors for the audience, its subtleties of orchestration were now tolerated by the players, and the work proved itself one of the best middle-of-the-road pieces of the new repertoire. Joseph Horovitz offered a neo-Straussian 'Ballet for Band' in 1983, contributing nothing new but delighting players and public, and Gregson provided one of his finest scores, 'Dances and Arias', in 1984. McCabe, shrugging off the general initial hostility to his early 'Images', achieved a popular vote with his beautifully scored, pastel-coloured 'Cloudcatcher Fells' of 1985, and Bourgeois returned with 'Diversions' in 1986, lighter and more ear-tickling than 'Blitz', but still testing for the players.

Since 1977, then, the policy of encouraging composers new to the contest scene – Bourgeois, McCabe, Horovitz,

Heaton, and the established Gregson – at the National finals must be accounted a big step forward. None of this repertoire is in any sense experimental or out of the way; all these composers would in a wider context be regarded as conservative, one even reactionary. The scores they have presented have, however, lifted music for contests out of the rut into which it had settled, away from debilitating attempts at Berlioz in transcription, forward into what must be regarded as almost another golden age, comparable with that of the 1920s and 1930s. They have given bands, it is hoped, a better taste in music, and an introduction to the art as it is actually being conceived by living composers at the end of the twentieth century, albeit conservative in idiom.

For conservative, tonal, amusing, charming and 'pleasant' it often is, and rightly so, bearing in mind the rehearsal commitment given over five or six weeks be enthusiasts who, though sometimes virtuoso in technical skills, yet remain cautious in their appreciation of modern music in general, and whose audience, on the two or three big days of the year, is looking for entertainment and emotional involvement in music it can understand. This new repertoire, then, has moved the band world forward in an acceptable way for composers, players and most audiences alike.

Much the same may be said for the European Championship, organized by the National and growing in significance. In its early years at the end of the 1970s, test-pieces had to be tailored to the wide disparity that existed between the competing bands in technical skills – the British bands being way ahead at that period. Several interesting works resulted, nevertheless, including Arthur Butterworth's malevolent scherzo 'Caliban'. The gap between the continental bands and the British has closed considerably over the decade, and the latest pieces are often as challenging as those for the National itself – Philip Sparke's 'Year of the Dragon' in 1986, for instance, and Michael Ball's 'Frontier' in 1987. An underrated piece from this list of commissions was Henk Badings' 'Ciaccona Seria' of 1983, but an inspired interpretation by Peter Parkes with the Black Dyke band revealed a serious and moving work.

It is time now to examine the second factor referred to,

the entertainment contest. When Granada Television presented the first Band of the Year Contest in 1971, it was an attempt to rejuvenate the programme repertoire of bands and to give them a chance to respond to the challenge of a neutral and difficult-to-please TV audience. Bram Gay, whose brainchild it was, had become, by the end of the 1960s, concerned and frustrated by the staleness of thinking in the band world; it was his idea to give ten bands twenty-five minutes each to play a programme of their own choice (plus one set piece) in front of the cameras. At first bands and their conductors reacted uncertainly, unaccustomed to such freedom of choice in a contest situation. It was obvious that the 'old' repertoire was of dubious merit in a television confrontation with rival bands, since although the live audience in the hall would respond, viewers might not. 'Stop them switching off in the first three minutes,' was the advice given by Arthur Taylor, producer of the programme for Granada: a new repertoire was needed.

An aspect of banding which had changed significantly since the early part of the century was the role played by the conductor-arranger, as mentioned in Chapter 6. By the middle of the century conductors had become primarily band trainers and contest specialists; now that there was a printed, comprehensive repertoire, there seemed less need for the conductor to arrange, and if he did, it was a bonus not a necessity. The Granada and later the Rothmans competition saw a redress of that balance; the bands most successful in these contests have been led by conductors with new ideas for programmes and arranging skills to match.

As it happens, I was one such, though this was unbeknown to Grimethorpe Colliery Band when they first engaged me to conduct them in 1972, the second year of Granada. There had been a cautious start the year before, the Cory Band winning with a traditional-style programme, well played. I decided to rethink all that I could remember about band programmes from some twenty years before, and do something different. Grimethorpe's programme in 1972 included Tudor music by John Bull, the set piece by Bryan

Kelly (a Novello composer), a dash of Glenn Miller, and an old warhorse from *Lohengrin* to finish; to begin, a virtuoso piece of light music which introduced an alter ego in the form of W. Hogarth Lear as composer. Grimethorpe won.

It was not exactly what Gay had intended – since there was an accent on lightness of style which, sadly, was too much copied in the following years – but it did set the scene for future composer-conductor-arrangers who have created a new repertoire, mostly of brilliant transcriptions from film and modernish orchestral scores. Little original music of any seriousness has resulted, and among traditionalists who resisted the idea in the first place there is a slightly holier-than-thou condescension towards what they regard as unseemly frivolity. The band movement is not without a degree of piety.

The band public in general, however, finds differently, and though such conductor-arrangers as Ray Farr, Denzil Stephens, Keith Wilkinson and Howard Snell has discovered composers and music it never expected to hear on brass: Stravinsky's *Firebird* Suite; various pieces of Shostakovich, including the Festival Overture; Hindemith's 'Metamorphoses of Themes of Weber'; Respighi's 'Pines of Rome'; and Ravel's second *Daphnis and Chloe* suite – all in arrangements which stretch scoring abilities and playing techniques beyond even the original test-pieces in some cases. So the old tradition has been revived, and two bands in particular have been given a very personal stamp: Grimethorpe, and Snell's Desford Colliery Dowty, whose libraries are as stuffed with new arrangements as Besses' and Black Dyke's are with old ones. Rimmer, Owen, Round and Greenwood, one senses, are nodding approval somewhere.

The last aspect of the changing repertoire is the one closest to my own heart and interests. I wanted to present bands to a wider serious public: to do so I needed programmes of original music, since I realized that the concert promoters would not be interested in arrangements even (or especially) of Stravinsky and Ravel. There was by now an increasing amount of quality original music, but here also was a problem. Original music for bands has, almost without exception, been commissioned for contest use.

From John Henry Iles onward the composer has thus been the servant of special circumstances; inspiring perhaps, but limiting, since the required length of each composition is always between ten and twelve minutes, anything longer being impractical, given the problems of marshalling bands to and from platforms and the extra time needed for the deliberations of the adjudicators. Even the best pieces, therefore, of both the old and the new original test-piece repertoire are short-winded, and programmes relying on them tend to lack a sense of flow: four such pieces do not necessarily make a good first half of a concert, and eight make for musical indigestion. If bands were going to perform away from their normal platform as well as to their local audience, which is what I, for one, wanted to see as part of a general 'change', two problems of the repertoire had to be faced – one of style and content, the other of length and continuity.

Several pieces had by 1972 been written for bands outside the contest culture, notably Thea Musgrave's 'Variations', composed for the Scottish Youth Brass Band in 1966, and Thomas Wilson's 'Refrains and Cadenzas', commissioned for the Cheltenham Festival of 1973 and played by the Black Dyke Mills Band conducted by Geoffrey Brand. Both pieces, especially Wilson's, gave at last to the repertoire a real taste of the twentieth century. It is fairly safe to say that, so far as is known, before these works no one had written music for bands which showed the influence of Bartók, Hindemith, Stravinsky or Schoenberg, the most influential composers of the early part of the century.[1]

A couple of bands, ambitious to find new audiences and willing to stretch themselves musically, decided to commission works from composers of uncompromising style. Grimethorpe approached Harrison Birtwistle. His 'Grimethorpe Aria' was first performed at the Harrogate Festival of 1973. The music is grim and bleak in mood – comfortless in its fierce yet plangent dissonance, slow-moving save for a few eruptive episodes. Birtwistle wrote

---

1 In fact I had, but all of it was unperformed. Brian Ferneyhough had written for band as a teenage bandsman, but the scores remain unseen.

parts for every player, though he omitted percussion. The multi-voiced instrumental aria (in the Gabrieli sense of canzona) was an entirely new solution to the problem of scoring for what were still the old forces: one soprano cornet in E flat, nine cornets in B flat, one flugel horn in B flat, three tenor E flat horns, two B flat baritones, two B flat euphoniums, three trombones, two E flat tubas and two BB flat contrabass tubas. Without tampering with the old formation, he discovered a new world of dense, wild, desolate sound unsuspected by traditionalists and not much to their liking. The piece has proved to be a great attraction outside band circles, as was intended; featured at the Proms in 1974, it has had regular performances at music festivals in the UK and abroad, both by Grimethorpe and other bands – mostly European or American.

Birtwistle suggested that Hans Werner Henze might be interested in writing for the same band. He was, and produced 'Ragtimes and Habaneras' in 1975: eleven epigrammatic movements, some miniature in scale, parodying more the old European band tradition than the British, which in any case he didn't know. Rumbas, tangos, curiously distorted in shape and harmony, including quotations from Mahler, Sigmund Romberg, Kurt Weill and others, should have made a sickly mélange, but Henze's wit and skill held together a potentially unstable confection. His solution to the scoring was similar to Birtwistle's, with individual parts for each player and with lots of muting effects providing maximum colour. This piece, too, was played at the Proms in the following year and has been very popular on concert tours in Europe and Australia.

A great capture was 'Garden Rain' by Toru Takemitsu, the Japanese composer. He had originally written the piece for the Philip Jones Brass Ensemble on their first tour of Japan in 1974. With his permission I transcribed it for brass band, and it was recorded along with the Birtwistle and Henze works for the Decca Headline Series in 1976. Takemitsu writes lyrical and romantic music which is harmonically complex; 'Garden Rain' became quite a favourite with several of the Grimethorpe players.

Another valuable transcription at that time, as the band

waited for the commissions to be written, was the Symphony for Brass and Percussion of Gunther Schuller. Schuller wrote the piece as a young man in the 1940s, when he was principal horn with the Metropolitan Opera House orchestra in New York. It is a brilliant tour de force of orchestral brass writing, quite unlike anything which had preceded it, and Schuller was happy for me to arrange it for the British-style band – a simple enough job since the tuba, trombone and trumpet (cornet) parts remain the same and only the four horn parts needed redistributing to the middle instruments of the band. The word 'symphony' had seldom appeared on brass band programmes, at least in genuine guise, discounting the old selections from classical or romantic orchestral scores. Schuller's piece proved its worth, being substantial in length, challenging to play and not too abrasive for middle-of-the-road audiences.

Composers, having heard these adventures into new territory, were not slow to respond, and in the next few years Grimethorpe premièred pieces by, among others, Anthony Payne – the robust yet passionate 'Fire on Whaleness', first performed at the York Festival in 1976 and maybe the most difficult score of all, but musically worth every moment put into its rehearsal; George Benjamin, whose 'Altitude' of 1977 was a brilliantly accomplished score by a brilliant young man, a pupil of Olivier Messiaen; Graham Williams, whose 'Paean' of 1976 was another virtuoso piece, sadly only performed once to date, with important soprano cornet and flugel horn parts; David Lumsdaine, who provided a difficult, brooding work – 'Eventide' - again only performed once so far, and then not convincingly as there were problems with the transpositions of the band parts which made for rehearsal difficulties and a shaky first performance. Michael Blake Watkins wrote a fine piece, 'Aubade', in 1973 which Grimethorpe played several times and which they revived in 1986. It deserves much wider performance since it is energetic yet poetic, with an important euphonium part in its middle section, and has interesting writing for all sections of the band.

Other bands were reluctant to follow Grimethorpe's lead, as there was a lot of criticism of these deliberately challenging scores in normal band circles. The one exception initially was the Besses o' th' Barn Band, which was conducted at that time by Ifor James, the horn soloist, and took a different tack, approaching rather more traditionalist composers but giving them a free hand. Graham Whettam wrote 'Partita' (1975–6) for Besses, and they premièred Frank Cordell's 'Spirals', a most interesting piece from the well-known film composer. Paul Patterson produced 'Chromascope' and later 'Cataclysm', which used some of the techniques of the Polish school of Lutoslawski and Penderecki; Besses gave the former at the Harrogate Festival in 1974. They developed, too, a relationship with Edward Gregson and encouraged him to write his Tuba Concerto, played by Besses and the great tuba virtuoso John Fletcher in 1976.

Grimethorpe continued in the meantime with H. K. Gruber, the Austrian composer, best known for his so-called pandemonium, 'Frankenstein!!', in which he sings and acts the principal part. Gruber was enthusiastic about writing for what was, to him, such a curious combination. He presented 'Demilitarized Zone', a dense score full of references to half-remembered (or forgotten) marches. It created an oddly illusory effect in performance – juggling with several strands of march tune at the same time produced great difficulties of balance during rehearsals – but the piece, though elusive, deserves more airings than it has received so far.

Before Gruber, and indeed earlier than most of the scores I have mentioned in this context, came two works by Derek Bourgeois. Bourgeois is a prolific composer, and as a former brass player retains an affection for the instruments. His output includes a brass quintet, a symphony for tuba and orchestra, a concerto for three trombones and several test-pieces for brass band. Although he was for a time musical director of the Stanshawe Band, his first two works for the medium were written for Grimethorpe: Concertos for Brass Band Nos 1 and 2. Both are substantial three-movement pieces of high virtuosity, vividly scored.

Unlike most of the scores written for Grimethorpe, they are in an accessible, approachable idiom, with tonal harmony not so far removed from that of, say, Gilbert Vinter, enabling players, conductors and audiences to respond favourably – at least, the progressives did, the diehards initially finding it hard going. The First Concerto is both amusing and exciting, quoting the 'Jamaican Rumba' of Arthur Benjamin in the first movement, elbowing Ravel heavily in the ribs in the second and being outrageous in the third, which is entitled 'The war-march of the ostriches' - Bourgeois has a heavily ironic tendency. Not so in the Second Concerto, which is rather more serious, leaning towards the heroics of Shostakovich, the scoring producing a huge sound from the conventional forces involved. This work was played at the Proms in 1981. Percussion in both pieces was important. He followed these two works with a third, concerto grosso style, for normal brass quintet – two trumpets, one french horn, one trombone and tuba – and band, which the Philip Jones Ensemble premièred with the Redbridge Youth Band, conducted by John Ridgeon, in 1976. This piece is very rarely performed, needing as it does professional players for the quintet, but it is an important addition to the repertoire and one which does need rediscovering soon.

Three other bands have notably encouraged commissions. The Yorkshire Imperial Metals Band under John Pryce-Jones initiated what is possibly Robert Simpson's best work for brass, 'The Four Temperaments', in 1982, and two works by Robin Holloway, 'Men Marching' and 'From the Hills and Valleys' (1981–2). Holloway, writing in his neo-romantic Strauss-like style, has provided in the latter piece a lengthy tone-poem of unabashed ardour – inspired by connotations from painting and poetry of the First World War. The music is very easily accessible to bands, mellifluous and tonal, and would suit the conducting style and temperament of several leading band conductors. It is surprising that so far they have not taken the plunge, contest training remaining overwhelmingly their number one priority. Pryce-Jones commissioned, too, Rupert Scott's 'The Fire of Life' in 1985. It is one of the most vehement and aggressive scores of this gifted composer and, again, needs further performances to establish it in the new repertoire.

Howard Snell's work as conductor-arranger with the Desford Colliery Dowty Band has seen remarkable results in entertainment competitions, but he has also instigated a policy of commissioning composers of a wide variety of styles to write for him. In 1985 he asked me for a new work and I wrote 'Music for Spielberg', a piece in five movements influenced by the films of the American film director Steven Spielberg. Along with another smaller piece of mine, 'Ascendit in coeli', it is the most satisfactory music I have so far written for brass band, though S'nell seemed to favour another piece of mine called 'The Bandsman's Tale'. To date he has also approached Chris Hazel, Ray Premru, Richard Arnell and David Blake for pieces. Robert Simpson has written 'Variations on a bass theme of Max Reger' for Desford, and Philip Sparke 'Variations on an Enigma', while John McCabe's 'Deserts II – Horizon', originally for the Philip Jones group, has been refashioned for brass band.

David Read of the Cambridge Co-op Brass Band has adopted a most remarkably enlightened policy with a band which is not quite in the first rank. They have proved that all the pickings need not go to the famous names, and have shrewdly chosen local composers who can help create interest in the area. Arthur Wills's 'Fenland Suite', which features a solo part for organ, has been a particular success, Wills being the present organist of Ely Cathedral.

The solo repertoire has not developed at quite the same pace. Gregson has written a cornet piece as well as his Tuba Concerto for band. His Horn Concerto (for orchestral horn) with band is a distinguished work too little performed, perhaps because traditionally bands expect soloists to be drawn from their own fraternity, not the professional world. My own Trombone Concerto has been performed in its band arrangement several times, and John Golland's Euphonium Concerto also finds its way into the occasional programme.

One of the most exciting new concertos, for solo trumpet and band, is by Chris Sansom, who wrote the piece for James Watson in 1978. It was premièred at the Scottish National Orchestra's prom series but was then neglected until 1985, when Sansom reworked what he regarded as an unsatisfactory first movement. Played by Håkan Hardenberger and Grimethorpe in a studio broadcast from Manchester before an invited audience, it made a stunning effect. It is lengthy – about twenty minutes long – in three movements, the middle of which is a long elegy for Duke Ellington, featuring the soloist on flugel horn with accompanying vibraphone. Sansom has also completed a work for solo piano and band – 'Double Entendre', of extreme complexity and difficulty, which awaits a first performance.

Electronic music has at last been coupled with a brass band. Robert Lennon, a former euphonium player, now composer-lecturer at the Electronic Studio in Accrington, has written a work for the Leyland Motors Band, who broadcast it in 1986. It is called 'Song of the Aristos' and features long cadenza-like passages for flugel horn and trombone combined with telling use of the electronics, with band and tape in a sometimes massive dialogue.

Finally, to complete this section, it is encouraging to note that Walton and Tippett, both at an advanced age, have graced the band repertoire, Walton with a re-orchestration of music he wrote in the 1930s for a Cochran revue – 'The First Shoot' – and Tippett with 'Festal Brass with Blues', incorporating some of the music from his Third Symphony. Walton's piece is towards his *Façade* style, amusing, slight, elegant: it was first performed at the Promenade Concerts at the Royal Albert Hall in 1981 by the Grimethorpe Colliery Band conducted by myself. Tippett's piece is dramatic and mercurial in the Festal sections and sombre in the Blues; it features a melancholy flugel horn and accompanying solo cornet. It was premièred by the Fairey Band in 1984 at the Hong Kong Festival, conducted by Howard Williams. Tippett's music for brass and bells, 'Praeludium', has also been arranged for band, by myself.

This new music, all in a genuinely mid-century idiom, has undoubtedly opened up new possibilities for bands and has solved some of the difficulties mentioned earlier. Programming does now have a much broader potential and so, consequently, does audience appeal, for although the normal band audience finds it difficult to relate to, say, Sansom or even Holloway, audiences elsewhere – in London, at the various music festivals, or abroad – have reacted with real pleasure to the wide variety of music that band programmes can now afford. The ten-minute test-piece need not hold sway when there are works of substance lasting twice as long, giving a different, less broken flow to the progress of a concert. Added to these original pieces, too, are full-scale arrangements now available to bands – Elgar's 'Enigma Variations' by Eric Ball, Respighi's 'Pines of Rome' by Howard Snell, Saint-Saëns' 'Carnival of the Animals' by Peter Reeve, and Mussorgsky's 'Pictures at an Exhibition' in my own arrangement, for instance.

Programmes in symphonic style are thus possible. Here are a few examples, almost at random:

John Ireland	—	Comedy Overture
Chris Sansom	—	Trumpet Concerto

INTERVAL

R. Vaughan Williams	—	Variations
Michael Tippett	—	Praeludium, arr. Howarth
Derek Bourgeois	—	Concerto for Brass Band No 2

Edward Gregson	—	Dances and Arias
Harrison Birtwistle	—	Grimethorpe Aria
Gustav Holst	—	A Moorside Suite

INTERVAL

Edward Elgar	—	Enigma Variations, arr. Ball

Arthur Bliss	—	Kenilworth
John Golland	—	Euphonium Concerto
Malcolm Arnold	—	Fantasy

INTERVAL

Modest Mussorgsky	—	Pictures at an Exhibition, arr. Howarth

As I remarked at the beginning of this chapter, it is far from clear exactly where the new repertoire will lead. Whether, in spite of the new programme possibilities, it will be much used by the bands remains to be seen, for clearly it cannot be forced on their normal public. Personally, I have never tried, since I would not wish to offend those whose sole musical interest bands are, and who find the culture shock of some contemporary music too severe, too high-brow. Like Everest, however, it is there, and I would repeat that there is an audience interested in it, and that there will be conductors, myself included, who feel a need to conquer it, and to express it.

10

Trombone Solo

A Conductor:
Major Peter Parkes

MAJOR PETER PARKES is Musical Director of the celebrated John Foster Black Dyke Mills Band. Their association began in 1975, since which time Major Parkes has established himself as the most successful contest conductor of the last decade. After joining the Army in the late 1940s, he took the bandmasters' course at its music college, Kneller Hall. He retired from the Army in 1979, having held a number of positions, including Director of the Band of the Grenadier Guards at Chelsea Barracks in London. Major Parkes lives near Doncaster, where Patrick Howarth talked to him in November 1986.

PATRICK HOWARTH: *Could you tell me something about your childhood, upbringing and general musical background? When did you start to play?*

MAJOR PETER PARKES: I come from Northampton, which is the South, really – it's only sixty miles north of London – and I did a great deal as a youngster. My father was an amateur musician, but he died when I was eleven, so beyond that time I was more or less on my own. The first thing I played was a bugle in the Boys' Brigade. Then, when I was thirteen or fourteen, I borrowed a violin and had lessons, though it was a bit late to start. Shortly after that I went into a band called the 'Old Comrades', a military band, which was run by a marvellous man called Fred Giddings, who was a trombone player in the Northamptonshire Yeomanry (TA) band. He'd always wanted to be a

165

conductor and, being quite a rich man, he basically bought his own band, and the Old Comrades used to rehearse over a pub which he owned. I was given a cornet first of all – I'd done some playing on brass instruments – but while I was there I tried a clarinet and found this suited me much better. So I was learning the violin and the clarinet. I carried on doing some playing on brass instruments, but it was mainly the clarinet.

PATRICK HOWARTH: *When did you get your first conducting experience?*

MAJOR PETER PARKES: When I was eighteen I had to join the Army; everyone did. I had four or five friends, all of them musicians – indeed, all of them later professional musicians – and one had joined early, before he had to, just to get into a band so he didn't have to be a soldier! This secmed like a good idea, and in fact we all joined early, because we all had to do National Service anyway. It wasn't intended to be a career for me, it was a stopgap. I had some idea about making a living from music and was playing the clarinet well, and the Army seemed like a short-term thing. But what happened was that when I joined the Army I was offered a course, which I took. Then I went abroad to Hong Kong, which I quite liked.

PATRICK HOWARTH: *Which regiment were you in?*

MAJOR PETER PARKES: The Royal Leicestershire Regiment, in the band. While in Hong Kong I was offered another course, a three-year course as a student bandmaster at Kneller Hall. By then I was a little tired of Hong Kong – I'd been there some time – so I accepted the course.

PATRICK HOWARTH: *Had you got your commission by this time?*

MAJOR PETER PARKES: No, I became a bandmaster. I did the three-year course in little over two – the Army was expanding at that time and I was allowed to jump a year.

I was fantastically lucky, because I was given a choice of bands, and the band that I went to was the Duke of Cornwall's Light Infantry, which was going to Jamaica and Bermuda. This was 1954, and it seemed like a pretty good way to spend the next three years. At the time I still had no idea about staying in the Army for a long time – by then I'd already been in for six or seven years. I was only twenty-five, very young for the job I'd got, so I went to Jamaica thinking it would be a nice three years. But one thing led to another. I had a fine band and we did a lot of touring all over the Caribbean. The regimental HQ was in Jamaica, with companies in Belize, Trinidad and Bermuda, and every year I had to visit them with the band, which was marvellous for me. I got a lot of musical experience out there, because we were the only music there was – I did *Les Sylphides* and *Swan Lake* with one violin, a piano, a set of drums and a military band! What a sound! I did the arranging, which was good experience. We also did backing for musical comedy in Bermuda.

I came back to England and then went out to Germany, changing bands a couple of times, and was then commissioned into the Royal Tank Regiment and took over their band from Arthur Kenney. From there I went to the band of the Royal

Engineers, which was possibly the best job I ever had in the Army. It was based in Chatham and was a very big band – seventy-five or eighty musicians, including about forty or fifty string players; they played other instruments as well, but to get into the band you had to play a string instrument as well as woodwind or brass. So we had a good orchestra and we could play music up to Brahms. We couldn't play anything really big, but could manage Sibelius up to a point, and were very good at Handel. We used to do super concerts. I was six years there.

From there I went to the Band of the Grenadier Guards, which I had for seven or eight years, and that was very glamorous, stationed in London at Wellington Barracks and latterly in Chelsea. The boys in the band had to be good to do the job; it was very demanding, but it wasn't always rewarding musically. You can understand why: the Army pays to have bands to provide music for occasions, but the music is of secondary importance – it's not as important as marching in straight lines. We played for banquets, or investitures or parades, so we spent most of our time marching up and down the Mall in a furry hat, which is OK; I enjoyed it.

The things about being a conductor in the army are: first of all, good training at Kneller Hall, spending two or three years training to be a conductor, being taught technique, everything. In fact, I don't think you *can* teach anybody to be a conductor. I've discovered this more and more teaching students – if they can already conduct, then you can help them, but you can't show them how to do it. I think it's a physical thing, like playing cricket. I can't play cricket, I can't catch a ball because of some lack of co-ordination somewhere, and I've seen conductors the same – they're never going to conduct as long as they live, while some people seem to find naturally that they can conduct and take charge of a band. The one thing the Army does give a conductor is a band. When I was with an infantry band I could do what I liked with them, within reason – I could conduct them for seven or eight hours a day. For twenty years I had a band at my disposal, and if I wanted an extra rehearsal I just did it; I gave the order and it was arranged. So you do get tremendous experience as a conductor.

PATRICK HOWARTH: *Have you found many similarities between training military bands and brass bands?*

MAJOR PETER PARKES: Well, no; there is a terrific difference. With the Guards, for instance, we were busy. In my last year with the Grenadiers we did over five hundred engagements – that includes everything from dance band to fanfare trumpet, from parades to concerts. There were about seventy-five musicians in the band, and every day the full band, or four or five sections of the band, were doing something different. There was a lot of responsibility and organization, but rehearsals were absolutely minimal. In the summer we used to play at the seaside, and you might be playing for seven or eight weeks but have only one rehearsal at the beginning. So you free-wheel. You're living on your fat. The playing is getting slicker, but losing any magic throughout the summer – it becomes like delivering milk. We used to play musicals like *The Sound of Music* or *Carousel* and I'd be off in a world of my own. I knew all the music, didn't need a score, just started it off and before I knew what was happening it had finished and we were saluting the public – I'd been thinking about gardening or holidays or something, nothing to do with music. Perhaps it does have something to do with professional music, where if you're not careful the music just becomes a job. I started music when I was thirteen or fourteen because I couldn't keep away from it – I had to make the connection myself, which is why I bought a fiddle. I went into it because I loved it, but if it just becomes a job, then it can be as boring and tedious as anything else, which is terrible. It didn't happen to me all the time, just with some aspects of the work. Sometimes you'd think: 'Dear me, this is nothing to do with music.' That's the danger of professionalism.

PATRICK HOWARTH: *But that doesn't happen with Black Dyke?*

MAJOR PETER PARKES: No. How I got Black Dyke Mills Band is crazy, because I'm a clarinet player – although not the first; there was Gladney, he took Dyke to first place at the Open five or six times. I couldn't have started with brass bands other than the way I did. I'd always wanted to. I went to the Albert Hall finals every year because I'd loved brass bands since I was a child. When I was a child Foden's were the band, and I heard Foden's in a concert and couldn't believe the quality of the playing. I still remember the first thing I heard them play, a march called 'Washington Greys', and still today whenever I play 'Washington Greys' I go back to that day and sound, which must have been terrific with Fred Mortimer conducting. So that was always with me, and when Harry and Alex Mortimer were working with bands I remember listening to them. But the opportunities weren't there. I was used to working with bands of a high standard, as most of them are in the Army, and I didn't really want to start at a low level, so it never happened.

But one day I had an incredible stroke of luck. I was in my office at Chelsea Barracks when the telephone rang and a fellow said: 'My name's Peter Lambert' (who I later discovered was an absolute brick as far as brass bands were concerned; he was president of Black Dyke Mills Band for about twenty-five years). 'My name's Peter Lambert, my company's got a little band and I wondered if you'd take it to a contest.' So I said: 'Which band is it and what's the contest?' And he said: 'It's Black Dyke Mills and it's the National.' He asked me if I'd like to think about it. I said: 'For about two seconds, yes!' Of course, I was absolutely delighted. This was in February 1975. I'd never conducted a brass band at all, so this was my first opportunity – right in at the top, which was the only way it could work for me. I was very fortunate.

PATRICK HOWARTH: *Had you followed the brass band world at all? Did you read the* 'British Bandsman'?

MAJOR PETER PARKES: Oh, yes. There are always three or four people in all Army bands who read the *British Bandsman* and they pass it around. So I was in touch with that. I'd followed

Alex Mortimer and the CWS Band in their great days in the 1950s and early 1960s. In fact, Alex used to take the band to London, to St James's Park, for a week every year, and most years I'd go along. And, as I've said, every year I went to the National contest at the Albert Hall. The year before, 1974, I'd watched Arthur Kenney and Cory win with Malcolm Arnold's 'Fantasy for Brass Band' – so I was in touch.

PATRICK HOWARTH: *Were many of the players in your bands from brass band backgrounds?*

MAJOR PETER PARKES: Yes. When I got Black Dyke ... what happened was that Geoffrey Brand had been professional conductor there, but then he became involved in the management of the National – he owned it, in fact – and couldn't do both, so he had to resign. They were looking for a professional, and I was on trial: I was given one contest. Fortunately we won it, so I was engaged for another, and it took off from there. But in my Guards band I had a fellow called Derek Greenwood (who until recently was director of the Camborne Band); he was absolutely brass orientated. And there was also Michael Dabbs, who I believe played the trombone in Grimethorpe Junior Band before joining the Guards. There were always some, about half a dozen, with a brass band background, but those two were real enthusiasts. So when I took over Black Dyke I had more respect from them for that than I did for being director of the Grenadier Guards.

I had brass bands in my blood all my life, but not at this level. You wouldn't in

Northampton – the nearest band to us was Munn and Felton's at Kettering, which became the GUS Band, a band I've always admired; and there was also Rushden Temperance nearby. But those names weren't as magical as Black Dyke and Foden's.

PATRICK HOWARTH: *How long did you carry on working with the two bands?*

MAJOR PETER PARKES: I did the National with Black Dyke in 1975, playing 'Une Vie de Matelot' by Robert Farnon, a marvellous piece, and we won it convincingly. The next year we got the double, with 'The Wayfarer' by Eric Ball at the National and Percy Fletcher's 'Epic Symphony' at the Open – two super pieces. And again the following year, with 'Connotations' by Gregson and 'Diadem of Gold'. So in my first five contests with Black Dyke we got a hat-trick of Nationals and two doubles of the Open and the National – no one's done that before, though it didn't seem to cause much of a stir. But it stirred me and it stirred the band; it won me their loyalty, and they've backed me ever since.

I found then that I was becoming more and more involved with brass bands. I still had to do my job with the Army, of course, but I found that all my thinking was with brass bands, almost from the first time I conducted Black Dyke. I stood in front of Black Dyke and I couldn't believe what I heard – the stick came down and there was a chord as big as a house; it was stupendous. It's one thing listening, but standing there and being responsible for it, hearing the sound and it happening when you want it to, that's a different thing altogether. I couldn't believe it. I couldn't stop smiling.

That was the big snag at first, because one of the things they used to say to me was, 'Major, you keep telling us we're good. Well, we know when we're good – we want to know when we're not.' That was only for the first couple of rehearsals, though. You've got to be very critical to conduct a band like that; you've got to hear what's wrong and put it right. There always is something wrong, no matter how good the combination is. There is always something that can be improved – in every bar there's something. This, I think, is where my success has been, such as it is: in being able to hear what's wrong, having a clear understanding of what I want to do with the music. My job as a conductor is to produce as near as possible what the composer wanted. Composers are not always right; sometimes I think their metronome marks don't work. But they must have a fairly clear idea of what they are trying to produce, and my job is not to re-compose, it's to interpret and to try to reproduce with the band what they've written, and to listen to the band and hear its weaknesses as well as its strengths. You have to hear both, or you can destroy its strengths.

Well, I haven't stopped smiling since 1975. What was there for me? I was an Army director of music and could have stayed there for another ten years. I retired ten years before I need have done. I'd have been a retired officer with a good career behind me, but I started a new life, and this is the most exciting thing I've ever done. I now can't leave it alone. My wife calls me a workaholic, but I'm not; I'm a musicaholic, or a bandaholic, if you like – just absolutely wrapped up in brass bands. Because – and I'm sure a lot of conductors find this – the most endearing thing about brass bands is that they want to do it. They want to rehearse, they want to get it right – you stop a thousand times in two hours, and as long as you're stopping for a good reason, they're with you. They never get tired, they are always prepared, they want every crotchet to be right. Well, that's what conductors want, too. So it's superb, really.

PATRICK HOWARTH: *When was it exactly that you left the Army?*

MAJOR PETER PARKES: I left in 1979.

PATRICK HOWARTH: *So you mixed the two for the first four years?*

MAJOR PETER PARKES: Yes. The Army was very good; they were delighted. My colonel was delighted because this was good public relations anyway. So it could have continued. When I say I was bored with certain things in Army music, that isn't to say that I didn't enjoy the Army, because I did enjoy it. I was very fortunate to have that chance of a career, and I owe the experience I have to a great extent to opportunities I had within the Army. But it had gone on a long time, I'd done everything ten times, and I could see nothing new ahead, so it was obviously time to change.

PATRICK HOWARTH: *So when you left the Army, were you then solely working with Black Dyke?*

MAJOR PETER PARKES: No. I was lucky, because I had a job in the end where I could organize my own time; I was at Aldershot. So what I did was use my last years in the Army to ease out of the one and ease into the other. By the time I left the Army I was involved in half a dozen bands, doing adjudicating; but if you looked at my diary for the year I left, you'd see more brass band than military band engagements. So I hardly noticed – the day I left I was busy. I must have had the easiest retirement from the Army that anyone has ever had, because the day I left I had a full diary for the next year. And within that year I went to Australia and New Zealand on two separate trips adjudicating.

PATRICK HOWARTH: *Can we talk specifically about Black Dyke for a while now?*

MAJOR PETER PARKES: I'm very proud to talk about Black Dyke.

PATRICK HOWARTH: *What is your role in the running of the band?*

MAJOR PETER PARKES: The company appointed me professional conductor to start with. The band has always had two conductors: a resident conductor who does the nuts and bolts – what used to be called bandmaster – and a professional. On the company payroll I am the Musical Director, but am still known as the professional conductor because that's the tradition.

PATRICK HOWARTH: *And it's Foster's who pays for you, is it?*

MAJOR PETER PARKES: Yes, that's right. Incidentally, the band is now called the John Foster Black Dyke Mills Band. John Foster joined the local band in 1819 as a French horn player. By profession he was a woollen cloth manufacturer. In 1837 he built his Black Dyke

The Hosepipe Symphony, as composed and performed by Elgar Howarth (far right)

Dennis Hussey

Saddleworth concerts   *Dennis Hussey*

Harry Mortimer conducting at *The British Bandsman* Centenary Concert, 1987   *Dennis Hussey*

Elgar Howarth and the Grimethorpe Colliery Band *Allied Artists*

Mills at Queensbury, and what more natural than that the village band should be associated with his company? 1987 saw the 150th anniversary of the band. After much discussion, the band's members decided to include John Forster's name in its title. The company has been very good; it has supported the band without any break, through bad times and good, for 150 years. So there's a terrific relationship there.

This business of having two conductors goes back to the middle of the last century. The first contest the band went to was the 1860 Crystal Palace, which they won, and the name hasn't been out of the records since. They have had periods when they haven't won the Open or the National for twenty years, but they've always had prizes. Besses are the only top-class band who have got a history to compare with it.

If you look at the names of my predecessors as professional conductor, they have all been there: Rimmer and Halliwell, Harry and Alex Mortimer, Geoffrey Brand. The resident conductors used to last a long time – twenty or thirty years, some of them, like Arthur O. Pearce. I've not been as lucky as that; we've had six in my eleven years.

PATRICK HOWARTH: *How important is your liaison with the resident?*

MAJOR PETER PARKES: Absolutely essential. It's a difficult job, resident. You can understand why I want to be a professional, I conduct the band at the big contests or on television and radio or on records – I get a certain amount of glory. The resident has to be an able conductor and musician. He does take the band to concerts and he does have some part to play in broadcasts and records, but he doesn't take the band to contests, so he doesn't have the same opportunities to make his name – or lose his name, it's just as easy to lose it. I think it's a good job, resident; in many ways it's preferable, because you're not under the same pressure.

PATRICK HOWARTH: *It must be the best stepping-stone in the band world, being resident at Black Dyke, if you want to go on to be a professional. Roy Newsome has certainly done well, for example.*[1]

MAJOR PETER PARKES: Yes, indeed, and Trevor Walmsley[2] and Derek Broadbent[3] have been with us.

PATRICK HOWARTH: *How many of the band work for Foster's nowadays?*

MAJOR PETER PARKES: None. I saw an article in a music magazine a few years ago, written by someone called Hector; he didn't know anything at all about brass bands, but managed to write a three-page article, so we get the wrong image with the public. He was talking about beer-bellies and about Black Dyke Mills – this band who work for this firm and have tea-breaks every other hour so they can rehearse in company time. At that time we had one person working for the mill, and he had a proper job. The cloth industry, being what it is, couldn't support parasites anyway.

1 Successful and respected conductor, now professional conductor of Williams Fairey Band and music director of the National Youth Brass Band (see Chapter 12)
2 Conductor of various bands, including Yorkshire Imperial Metals Band, in the 1970s
3 Well-known band trainer and arranger of Brighouse and Rastrick's chart hit 'The Floral Dance'

Never in the existence of Black Dyke Mills Band have they been in a position where they could rehearse in company time. Never. Anyone who has worked for the firm, as far as I know and as far as anyone has told me – and they can remember quite far back – has had a real job. But in my time with the band we have only had about three or four working there, and none of those does now.

PATRICK HOWARTH: *What sort of occupations do the bandsmen have now?*

MAJOR PETER PARKES: We have a few peripatetic brass teachers. We've got a fellow who's a long-distance lorry driver, and a gas board engineer. John Clough, the euphonium player, is an organ builder; he helped to put the organ into York Minster. We've got painters and decorators – everything, really. We've got a few fellows involved in the cloth-weaving industry, as you might expect, although not with Foster's, but with other firms. Schoolmasters, several students.

PATRICK HOWARTH: *How difficult is it for them to fit their jobs around playing with the band?*

MAJOR PETER PARKES: It's not easy. One of the differences between Black Dyke and some other bands is the commitment. A journalist friend of mine wrote an article a few years back and he said, 'This band, Black Dyke, appears to do very little.' At the time I was very annoyed and I wrote him a letter, which I didn't send, actually; but I looked at the band diary for the previous year, and we'd done fifty-five concerts, one hundred and forty rehearsals, made two or three LPs, done three broadcasts and

three contests and a two-week tour, so it
worked out that out of 365 days in a year
we had worked over 200, not full days, but
200 days of commitment. That's more than
most people do for their job, and this is
supposed to be an amateur band.

At Black Dyke at 7.30pm everyone's in
his chair – unless someone is really ill, no
one is absent. At most bands you can find
four or five empty seats, and the players
are absent for very good reasons, but those
excuses would not be accepted at Black
Dyke. We've had more than one or two
good players who have changed their jobs
and couldn't come to rehearse every other
Monday, for instance, and they have had
to leave the band. The band won't accept
anything other than total commitment –
the minute it does, it will become just like
any other band.

PATRICK HOWARTH: *How hard is it to deal with and work with
the incredible Black Dyke tradition? You
must have been very aware of it when you
started to work with them.*

MAJOR PETER PARKES: Yes, I was, of course. Somebody said:
'Does it make you feel very humble?'
Well, that's the last way you should feel;
these are very touchy people, if you show
them any humility they'll eat you! You
have to be very confident and know what
you're doing – if you make a mistake, they
don't forgive it. We had one resident
conductor who only lasted three weeks.
It's a tough job. However, it suits me; I
love the job. I even enjoy the rows we
have – it's all part of living. But you have
to be aware of the band's past: my ambition has to be to leave the band at least as
good as when I took over, and we haven't

changed the traditions. This is nothing to do with being old-fashioned. It's not all 'Labour and Love' – I love modern music. Black Dyke has an image of being very traditional. When I was in Sweden recently a Swedish conductor told me that he had been told that Black Dyke was very good at contests but no good at concerts. That's absolute nonsense. We fill every hall we perform in at concerts – you hardly ever see empty seats – and that is because the band is geared to entertainment. We are traditional because we have an image we have to support, of being the finest brass band there is, so you won't see Black Dyke wearing funny noses or shaking maracas.

PATRICK HOWARTH: *But this traditional image still encompasses performing the modern repertoire?*

MAJOR PETER PARKES: Yes, that's the point. If you look at the record of contests we've entered in the last ten years, we have won seventeen out of thirty of them and come second on seven or eight occasions. If you look at the contests we have won, they have been with the big epic modern pieces. We don't do well with a piece that doesn't test the band, which has happened lately when the pieces have been light music and one band sounds very much like another. If you get a piece like Derek Bourgeois' 'Blitz' or Robert Simpson's 'Volcano', then the difference between bands comes out. 'Volcano', for instance, is shaped like a symphonic first movement and so the band is concentrating flat out for ten minutes. A lot of bands find this difficult as compared with a suite of three or four short movements, where your concentration can lapse.

So this business about the band being traditional – yes, it is traditional and the standards expected are high, but it's not old-fashioned.

PATRICK HOWARTH: *How do you go about maintaining such high standards?*

MAJOR PETER PARKES: When a player auditions for a place in the band, he is auditioned by the band. Everyone has to play a solo, attend a few rehearsals and sit in at two or three concerts, by which time the band know whether he is going to fit in or not – whether he is going to take it seriously.

PATRICK HOWARTH: *How many people will audition to fill a vacant chair?*

MAJOR PETER PARKES: It depends. Sometimes we don't fill a vacancy of ages. We had a vacancy for a B flat bass which we didn't fill for three years, because we could not find the right person. We used deputies and temporaries for some time, because the worst thing you can do is act in haste – once you let them in, they become difficult to dislodge. The standard goes down almost without noticing.

Some things are difficult, though. We were talking earlier about how many bandsmen worked for the company. Well, when I first went there in 1975, the economic climate was not as bad as it is now, and if I wanted a player from Wales in the band we could give him a job temporarily while he looked around for a job. These days we have to rely on players from Yorkshire or Lancashire; we cannot go farther afield unless the player can find himself a job.

PATRICK HOWARTH: *Can you tell me something about your preparation for the National or the Open Championships?*

MAJOR PETER PARKES: We generally get to know about the test-piece for Belle Vue in late June, whereas the National test-piece will not come through until late July. First of all we run the piece through. We give the parts out to the players, who then go off on holiday for two or three weeks, and so we don't begin serious rehearsal until the middle of August. The resident conductor takes the first rehearsal as a rule, and he arranges sectional rehearsals for the cornets, trombones, baritones and so on. He makes sure that every member of the band takes part in at least one sectional rehearsal. Then we rehearse the piece flat out, and we have two rehearsals a week with the full band during the last two weeks of August, which I take. Then we have the double rehearsal – two rehearsals on the Sunday before the contest, then every day for the last week.

PATRICK HOWARTH: *Are these the public rehearsals of the test-piece before setting off for a contest?*

MAJOR PETER PARKES: All our rehearsals are public; we have a dozen or so chairs in the band room and anyone can come to listen. The only people not allowed in are competing bands.

We rehearse Monday and Tuesday and generally have the big public rehearsal on the Wednesday before a contest in the Victoria Hall, Queensbury.

PATRICK HOWARTH: *Will you get a big crowd for that?*

MAJOR PETER PARKES: One or two hundred people, depending

on what the piece is, and how the band is playing. But we always get a good crowd, many of whom will be ex-members of the band, like Peter McNab, who has very firm ideas about whether a thing is right or wrong. For instance, this year with the 'Epic Symphony': he said we'd get nowhere with that, it was too slow. It makes you think, it gives you a bit of feedback. In fact, he was right, because what I was trying to do was stretch it and see just how it was phrased. It's marvellous having a public rehearsal, because you get to hear the piece in another room and get a public reaction. That's one tradition I've never changed.

PATRICK HOWARTH: *Do the local people of Queensbury attend?*

MAJOR PETER PARKES: Oh, yes, they come along.

PATRICK HOWARTH: *Is there much loyal local support?*

MAJOR PETER PARKES: They are certainly interested. Once, you would get coachloads of people coming from all over the country, in fact this year we had a coach party of fifty turn up.

Moving the day of the National from Saturday to Sunday has ruined our best tradition. If we won the National we would stay in London on Saturday night and have a party, fill that cup!

The next day we get to Queensbury at dusk and march into the town – well, Black Dyke can't march, but we have a shot at it – with four of the old-timers proudly carrying the cup in front of us. We march to the Victoria Hall, playing our own march, which is called 'Queensbury', and once there we give a concert to the local people. It's a very happy occasion and an admirable tradition.

We have a private rehearsal on the Thursday or Friday after the Victoria Hall public rehearsal. No one is allowed into this one, and this is when we swear at each other and so on. It's always most useful, because we usually find something we've missed out. For instance, this year with Howard Blake's 'Fusions' – it started out as the only piece for the Open, and then Harry Mortimer decided to add two movements of the 'Epic Symphony', because some people thought that the test-piece wasn't difficult enough. When you look at the score it's quite sparse, there are no black pages, nothing too technically difficult. But the more you practise it, play it, perform it, the more difficult it becomes – it's one of those pieces. We'd pulled it apart and studied every crotchet, every semiquaver, put it back together again, and although we had the balance and the tempos, there was no magic. At the public rehearsal I felt that it wasn't quite there, but at the private rehearsal on the Friday night it suddenly came right, and it was one or two things that happened in the concentration of that rehearsal which put it right. That's another good tradition for you.

We have a rehearsal on the day itself, when we play one or two hymn tunes and look at a few danger spots in the test-piece, but we don't play it right through on the day itself. I do with other bands, but Black Dyke have more experience of playing to large audiences than most, so they don't get as nervous. We just play a few hymn tunes as smoothly as possible, to get the balance and the intonation right.

PATRICK HOWARTH: *Can I ask you why Black Dyke have always been so reluctant to enter entertainment contests?*

MAJOR PETER PARKES: There's a very good reason for that. We've got democracy at Black Dyke. The conductor doesn't make all the decisions other than musical ones, and the band itself decides upon engagements – the whole band is on the committee. I remember I had to work like blazes to convince the band that the European Championship was a good thing to enter; they didn't want to go originally. When it comes to entertainment contests it's the same thing – the band decides. Black Dyke feels that these contests cannot be taken seriously: all the bands play different music, it's always open adjudication and, judging from past results, it's not always the best band which wins – often the most entertaining, perhaps, but not always the best. So Black Dyke likes a traditional contest, where you've been set the music you have to play and then you have to make that music work with closed adjudication. I personally think that any sort of open adjudication is daft.

The other thing I feel personally is that, although entertainment competitions have done a lot of good, they have not done what they set out to do. The original aim of the entertainment contests in the mid-1970s was 'to further the cause of brass band music'. But the bands don't play brass band music in these contests. A famous band and its conductor will prepare a piece for a contest, and then they can't use it again. The piece may be passed down to some other bands, but then it will

be lost. It's like a treadmill for music. For
instance, if you played Shostakovich's
'Festival Overture' eight or nine years ago,
it was exciting music, but now if you play
it, it's old hat. How can it be old hat when
it's still fine music? Desford have performed some excellent music, but the
minute they start to play something more
than three or four times people begin to
say they're losing it, they're no good any
more. Another thing is that if you look at
the last nine or ten years of Black Dyke,
we've been National or Open champions
nearly every year, and sometimes European champions as well, so we don't need
to prove anything. We've got nothing to
gain from them, and everything to lose.

PATRICK HOWARTH: *You did say that you thought entertainment contests had done some good. In what
ways, do you think?*

MAJOR PETER PARKES: They have broadened the repertoire,
and they have brought in a new audience.
Some of the traditional brass band audiences do actually enjoy listening to a
test-piece twenty times, and judging it
themselves. Another section of the public
is not quite this interested – perhaps they
don't understand it, they want to be
entertained – and I hope the entertainment contests are attracting this audience.
Personally, I am a test-piece conductor. I
like conducting an original piece for band
and trying to get the best performance that
anyone may ever get of it. I can't do that
with Tchaikovsky arranged for band, because it's always been done better before
by an orchestra, for one thing. I am not
against it – I spent most of my life
arranging music for odd musical combina-

tions – but I prefer the original music for band, and so do Black Dyke. It's as simple as that.

PATRICK HOWARTH: *Which bands other than Black Dyke have you worked with?*

MAJOR PETER PARKES: I've taken Grimethorpe to the area contests and the Miners' Contest a few times, and that's a marvellous band to work with.

PATRICK HOWARTH: *What do you feel are the differences between Black Dyke and Grimethorpe?*

MAJOR PETER PARKES: I don't think there are many differences. They've both got the same sort of sound – big, rich, old-fashioned sounds. They've got slightly different approaches – perhaps they are not quite so serious at Grimethorpe. Their sound is perhaps a little lighter than Dyke's. I am not really sure what the basic differences are but they are one of the great bands.

I worked at Fairey Engineering for three years and we were quite successful. They've got a much lighter, brighter sound. It's interesting that you have all the same instruments but can produce a noise of different quality with each band. Fairey's sound is very distinctive – no other band sounds quite like Fairey's.

I have been professional adviser to Whitburn Band for seven years and we have won the Scottish Championship five or six times together. We went 'pot-hunting' together one year, for fun, and we won eighteen consecutive contests in Scotland. We did it to get the band off the ground; to instil into everybody a sense of occasion and stage experience.

I have been with the Ever-Ready Band

for five years now. They are on their own, really, up in the North-East, but they are a good band. If you get all the big bands together at the National or the Open, Ever-Ready always do well.

PATRICK HOWARTH: *Do you ever conduct more than one band at a contest?*

MAJOR PETER PARKES: Oh, yes, sometimes. I have been connected with the City of Coventry Band, which is now the Jaguar Band, and one year I took them and Ever-Ready to Pontin's, and took first and second – the band that was second didn't like it much!

PATRICK HOWARTH: *Do you ever take anyone else along with Black Dyke?*

MAJOR PETER PARKES: I can't. In my contract with Black Dyke I am not allowed to take or prepare another band for a contest for which I am entered with Black Dyke. But I wouldn't want to anyway.

PATRICK HOWARTH: *Are Black Dyke happy for you to work with other bands as long as it doesn't impinge on your commitment to them?*

MAJOR PETER PARKES: They weren't at first. But there are advantages, because I get to know what the standards are elsewhere, which helps me assess Black Dyke's strengths and weaknesses. Black Dyke have said that I am showing other bands their secrets and methods, but I think my job as a conductor is to work with bands and make them as good as they can be. But Black Dyke are actually very generous-minded, I think.

PATRICK HOWARTH: *To finish, may I ask you a few general questions? Are there any bands and conductors from the past or present that you particularly admire?*

MAJOR PETER PARKES: I admire all the people who put so much time into brass bands. Even in the most successful bands the money they get is peanuts. Black Dyke work a couple of hundred days a year, as I've told you, but many bands work just as hard. After a concert or a contest people may go on about how marvellous a conductor is, but he hasn't had to play a note, he hasn't had to hit a top C. No, it's the players who do it, it's they whom I respect.

Having said that, the conductor is terribly important. There are half a dozen top professional conductors, but then there is a gap. There may be any number of people who can do a fair job, but that's not good enough. I feel we need some sort of training system – desperately, in my opinion – to encourage good young talent.

PATRICK HOWARTH: *What other changes or innovations do you feel are necessary?*

MAJOR PETER PARKES: The first and most important is controversial. In the last three or four years I have become involved in the National Federation of Brass Bands, which has a number of associations around the country, through which bands are members of the Federation. There are about 960 contesting bands who are members, and I should like to see those bands giving reasonable financial support to the Federation each year. I should like to see the bands owning and running the big championship themselves. Brass bands need to ensure their own survival. In a world where entertainment is going to play an increasingly important part in people's lives, bands can play an important role. But we are still living in the past, organizing contests with £20 as first prize. We ought to try to get away from this image of always seeming to be hard up. If nearly a thousand bands gave £50 each, they would be going a long way towards becoming self-supporting. We might even have a brass band office with a full-time executive officer!

Next, adjudication. I think adjudication is often badly done. We bring in big names from other branches of music to adjudicate. But if, for instance, I were asked to adjudicate at the Three Choirs Festival, I would turn it down, choral music is not my sphere of expertise. If your tap is dripping you send for a plumber. We keep sending for electricians to do the plumbing, and that's got to be daft. The bands work hard to get to the highest standards for contests and they deserve to be judged by people who know and love the sound.

11
Medley

A Wider World

THIS CHAPTER LOOKS at a number of areas which are not directly concerned with British brass banding but which have important links with the movement. In particular it discusses military bands, the Salvation Army, brass bands overseas, education, popularity, and the role of women in the band world.

As we have seen, military bands played an important part at the inception of the brass band movement, being a source of both players and instruments, but generally the two areas of music-making have remained independent of each other. The connections that do exist between them are still based on players. Many military bandsmen have come from a brass band background – advertisements for musical recruits often appear in the *British Bandsman,* and at a time of mass unemployment some find an army career quite an attractive prospect. Similarly, some bandsmen will return to civilian banding after their army service is finished.

Musically, the two traditions have less in common. Military bands are basically wind bands, different from brass bands in that they include woodwind instruments as well as brass. Nor do military bands compete in organized contests in the way that civilian brass bands do. The repertoire of the military band has had its effect on brass bands from the very beginning. It is no coincidence that the march is the style of music most generally associated with brass bands, but although military bands do have their own repertoire, most notably Sousa and other American writers for wind band, there is much less exciting new music for wind band than for brass band. It is not too surprising that the adventurous innovations of the civilian bands are not reflected by their military counterparts, for military bands are units which operate to provide accompaniment for occasions rather than playing for themselves – in some respects they are more to do with looking correct and marching nicely than performing music.

One facet of military banding that could be usefully copied by the brass bands is the amount of instruction that they give to their conductors and band trainers. At the army's Kneller Hall School of Music or the Royal Marines School at Deal, Kent, or at RAF Uxbridge, young service musicians receive an excellent musical training. Opportunities are also considerable: the army alone has over seventy regimental bands, as well as orchestras and other groups. At a time when some people in the·brass band world are bemoaning the shortage of top-class conductors, such programmes could be more widely copied – the success of ex-army conductors like Major Arthur Kenney or Major Peter Parkes speaks well for the value of their training.

Links between brass bands and the Salvation Army are perhaps closer than those with military bands. After all, both are purely brass-format bands, and some of the origins of Salvationist music lie in· the history of brass bands. Charles Fry and his three sons, Fred, Ernest and Bert, are credited with being the first Salvation Army band when they played at a meeting in Salisbury in 1878. Charles had been solo cornet in the 1st Wiltshire Volunteer Rifle Corps – as mentioned earlier, many brass bands had become Volunteer Movement bands in the 1860s. (Many brass bands were also involved in the Temperance Movement, which had affiliations with Salvationism.) It is natural that a religious organization concerned with the spiritual needs of the man in the street should become interested in bands, since brass bands themselves were supposed to be attractive to ordinary people. However, William Booth, the founder, was sceptical about using music at early Salvationist gatherings, despite the historical associations between music and religion; but when he realized that the music attracted people to the religion he softened his opinions, although it has always been stressed that Salvation Army bandsmen are Christians first, Salvationists second and musicians third. Even today, musicians in the top corps bands, such as Chalk Farm and

Regent Hall in London, or the International Staff Band, the central Salvation Army band, hold this maxim close to their hearts.

The Salvation Army has always remained independent from the secular banding movement – in particular the bands do not enter competitions and they have their own repertoire, which is fiercely guarded and only rarely lent out to secular bands. The main links between the two banding worlds are again through personnel, with many top bandsmen gaining their training in the Salvation Army before joining secular brass bands. Although Salvation Army repertoire is uniquely its own, some of the leading Salvationist composers have written for brass band, most notably Eric Ball, a former Bandmaster of the International Staff Band and one of banding's best-loved figures. Just like brass bands, Salvation Army bands often play in parks or at the seaside, and they were also once regular performers on the radio, although these appearances have dwindled as the number of opportunities have diminished. Unlike secular banding, the Salvation Army has a very strong centralized organization – as all Christian institutions have – part of which looks after music. The Music Department was set up by Booth as early as 1883 and protected the Salvation Army's publishng interests. In 1921 a National Secretary for Bands was appointed, who had a whole team of officials under him (including a band inspector to advise bandmasters on technical problems) to look after the bands and their activities. Perhaps the brass band movement could learn something from the Salvationists here?

Probably the most important contribution that the Salvation Army has made to the wider world of banding is in its work overseas. The Household Troops band had toured America and Canada in 1888–9, and Holland in 1891. (Sousa had met William Booth on several occasions and knew that the Salvation Army bands had played an important role in the spreading of music – so impressed was he that in the early 1930s he wrote a march, 'The Salvation Army', especially for the movement.) The Chalk Farm Corps Band toured Europe extensively during the first part of the twentieth century, spreading both the word of salvation and the sound of brass. By the end of the nineteenth century the Salvationists had travelled to virtually all parts of the world, taking their music with them. Captain and Mrs Thomas Sutherland, for instance, arrived in Adelaide in 1881; the Captain soon founded the Adelaide 1 Band, and later started the influential Sydney Congress Hall Band. Salvation Army operations began in New Zealand in 1883, and nine months later four or five fully equipped bands took part in Salvationist celebrations. Similar activity was taking place in Europe. In Norway there had been no brass band cult; many had not heard such music until they became Salvationists, according to Klaus Østby, a pupil of Grieg's and an important Salvationist musician. Sweden's flourishing band movement is almost completely based on a Salvationist background. The exportability and development of brass banding overseas is one of the most interesting and potentially most exciting facets of the band movement today, and there seems no doubt that it owes much of its success to the Salvation Army's pioneering work.

However, it should be remembered that secular bands toured and secular bandsmen emigrated, and this social influence must be examined in conjunction with the religious influence of the Salvationists. Britain had been sending out settlers to the outposts of her empire throughout the nineteenth century; some of these people had taken their love of brass bands with them. This trend had continued just as energetically into the early twentieth century, by which time brass bands had taken a firm grip upon the affections of the British working class. Today emigrants to Australia or New Zealand find a healthy and well-organized banding scene ready for them to fit into. Overseas banding is strongest in the Antipodes, where early settlers had founded bands as early as the 1880s. In 1980 New Zealand celebrated the centenary of national brass band contesting in Christchurch. These national contests are even bigger affairs than the British National Championships. They last five days, incorporating solo and quartet contests and, for full band, 'own-choice', hymn tune, set test-piece, street parade and quickstep and marching contests, the last of which involve fiendishly difficult set manoeuvres while playing. The overall champion is computed from the aggregate scores from the 'own-choice', test-piece and march sections. Both countries also have democratically elected central organizing bodies who determine contest policy and rules, and oversee the banding movement generally.

Australia and New Zealand led the world in sending their bands abroad. It was a tour by the Hinemoa Band from New Zealand in 1903 which encouraged John Henry Iles to organize tours for Besses o' th' Barn. The National Band of New Zealand, which is formed every four years to go on a world tour of some months' duration, has been a regular visitor to Britain, and during its first tour in 1953 had the temerity to win the British Open. Australian bands have also visited Britain, but perhaps that country's most notable export was the conductor, arranger and celebrated cornet soloist Frank Wright, who came to England in 1934, toured with the St Hilda Colliery Band, and soon established himself as a popular figure in the British band movement – an interesting example of a citizen of a former colony returning to the 'old country' to show them how it's done.

The other Commonwealth country with a brass band tradition is Canada, although the band scene is much quieter and is naturally more influenced by the wind band tradition of America. However, the Kinsmen International Band Festival at Moose Jaw, founded in 1972, includes brass bands among its many popular attractions.

The enthusiasm for banding in the Commonwealth, and more recently in Europe, owes much to the touring of certain bands whose performances demonstrated just how good brass bands could be and how good the fledgling foreign efforts could become with practice. The most famous tour was that of Besses o' th' Barn in 1906, which included visits to America, Canada, Honolulu, the Fiji Islands, New Zealand and Australia. Black Dyke had in fact preceded Besses across the Atlantic by a few months, and both bands were to tour in Europe, particularly Holland and Belgium, in later years. Today many bands have visited Europe – according to the *British Bandsman* nearly fifty British bands toured abroad in 1984 – but trips farther afield are more difficult to finance, and at the time of writing it seems no

British band will be able to travel to Australia for the World Championship in 1988.

European banding has probably been the greatest beneficiary of all this activity abroad, and today many European countries have burgeoning brass band movements. Events such as the European Championship, which was founded in 1978, have encouraged continental involvement in British banding activities. The Swedish bands Solna and Limmhamms have both toured in Britain; Danish conductor Herbert Møller has twice been guest conductor on National Youth Brass Band courses; a Dutch band competed at the Granada and other Dutch enthusiasts are regular visitors to the National Festival in London. Conversely, British banding expertise is much in demand abroad, with people travelling the world as conductors, adjudicators and band trainers. Bands seem especially popular with the young abroad: Belgium, Switzerland, Australia and New Zealand all have national youth bands, and other countries are following suit. Apart from the countries mentioned above, Luxembourg, the Faroe Islands, Iceland, Norway and Germany all have the beginnings of a brass band movement.

The USA, of course, has a strong banding tradition of its own, but these are wind bands, featuring woodwind as well as brass instruments, like our military bands – most of Sousa's brilliant marches were written for this larger instrumentation. British-style brass bands remain relatively unknown, although tours such as Cory's and Grimethorpe's in 1976 have been enthusiastically received. However, a brass band course was held at the University of North Carolina in 1980, and by 1982 there were four bands in the state. Peter Wilson, editor of the *British Bandsman,* and others have been on lecture tours to explain and promote the movement, but as yet it remains a cult, although a growing one. The most surprising area of banding activity is possibly Japan, where by 1981 there were already at least twenty-two bands, including the exotically named Band of the Black Colt from Tokyo. A tour by Leyland Vehicles Band, with their conductor Richard Evans, and Harry Mortimer, to give both concerts and master-classes, was

198 WHAT A PERFORMANCE!

instrumental in encouraging this ever-increasing interest.

There can be no doubt that brass banding is fast proving itself to be one of this country's most valuable cultural exports. There are those who believe that new ideas and activities may well come from the Continent and that it won't be too long before the European Championship, dominated so far by British bands – Black Dyke in particular – may go across the North Sea. Some European bands are already giving the British a run for their money, so an upset may not be too far off. European banding is not hampered by a class problem such as exists in Britain. There is no cloth-cap image on the Continent; rather, brass bands are a growing cult which anyone feels able to get involved in, regardless of profession or social status. The *British Bandsman* already reports on championships in Belgium, the Netherlands, Switzerland, Norway, Denmark, Sweden, North America, Australia and New Zealand, as well as on Northern Ireland's independent championships, and if contests raise standards abroad as they do here, then foreign bands will soon be a major competitive and musical force to be reckoned with.

If brass banding is becoming more and more popular overseas, the same cannot be said of Britain. The hard core of banding enthusiasts remains as constant as ever, and although some have strongly resisted innovation, especially musical innovation, the majority have proved to be adaptable and fairly open-minded. The wider audience has been less loyal, but not surprisingly so.

The golden days of brass band radio were the 1940s and 1950s when, thanks to the persistence of Harry Mortimer and Denis Wright, bands were appearing up to sixteen times a week on the BBC. However, while this reflected brass bands' undeniable popularity at the time, it also reflected a relative lack of programming variety. The 1960s brought us the Beatles and the subsequent pop music explosion, which began to squeeze out the less popular styles from the airwaves, including the by now distinctly old-fashioned-looking brass bands. Not surprisingly, available air-time began to decrease, so that today bands are lucky to get three slots a week on BBC Radio. Local radio, however, has proved an area of expansion and, especially in more traditional banding areas, local bands are enjoying a reasonable amount of exposure.

Television has proved even less well disposed towards bands. The BBC *Best of Brass* competition was taken off the air because of bad audience ratings, though it returned in a non-competitive form; but some band enthusiasts were never enthusiastic about that show. A new BBC contest, *Champion Brass*, has been started, but is only shown in the North-East and North-West regions. Granada Television have perhaps been the greatest champions of bands, but even they experience difficulty in selling their televised contest to any regions which don't appear to have a traditional band audience. The Granada producer Arthur Taylor, a leading student and enthusiast of the band movement, has been responsible for the best coverage. His programme *Arrivederci Grimethorpe*, covering the colliery band's visit to the Montepulciano Festival in Italy in 1979, showed a top band far removed from its accepted environment, playing interesting and entertaining music, but even this programme was aired late at night, presumably because the schedulers didn't think many people would want to watch it. If more imaginative work was made, like Taylor's film, rather than the usual contest programmes, which are satifying neither as contests nor as television, brass bands might find a niche in television programming as subjects of cultural, human and documentary interest.

The record industry and brass bands have had a very long-standing partnership. Black Dyke were recording 78s as early as 1904, Besses a year later; however, these early recordings are now lost, although some collectors may have them. Contest success has generally led to recording contracts, performances of test-pieces being especially popular, such as Irwell Springs' 'Labour and Love'. Foden's, the most successful band of the 1930s, recorded a large number of 78s, as did their star solo cornet player Harry Mortimer, sometimes in partnership with Jack Mackintosh. These early 78s are often all we have left of some famous bands like St Hilda's, Horwich RMI and the Carlisle St Stephen Band, but it is impossible to guess how many were released, although the number is probably quite high, and the discs themselves are now eagerly sought by collectors. After the Second World War, the market for records rapidly increased, resulting in some bands signing long-term contracts; for instance, CWS (Manchester) and Alex Mortimer released over twelve LPs in ten years for Fontana, a subsidiary of Phonogram. The 1960s saw even greater expansion and a steady output of releases from GUS (Footwear) Band and Stanley Boddington on Columbia Records, Harry Mortimer's All-Star Brass on Paxton and Decca Records, and Black Dyke Mills in the EMI Music for Pleasure 'Listen to the Band' series. However, since 1970 the number of releases has steadily decreased, although there have been influential records by Black Dyke on RCA, by GUS on EMI and by Grimethorpe on Decca. Today few major recording labels are interested in brass bands, but bands have continued to record for smaller labels such as Chandos and Twoten. Some releases even sell quite well – for instance, Philip McCann's recent album of cornet solos; and Black Dyke are available on compact disc with their performance of Derek Bourgeois' 'Blitz'.

The most popular brass band record of recent years, and perhaps of all time, was Brighouse and Rastrick's 'Floral Dance'. As we have already pointed out, much of the publicity resulting from this success was negative, since it merely reinforced the popular image of bands as men in mock military uniforms playing trite music. Until the media are prepared to treat brass bands with the respect they deserve, the typical brass band picture in the national press will be of a coal-covered miner playing the euphonium or a little boy or girl trying to carry a B flat bass – wider popularity seems unlikely, because the greater public will continue to regard brass bands as a pleasant nostalgic oddity.

The importance of education to the future of banding has been mentioned elsewhere, but cannot be emphasized too strongly. If bands are to keep their existing audience, then that audience needs constant replenishment with new blood, and the young players often introduce their parents and friends to their banding activities, which helps to expand the wider following. What is especially encouraging is that the availability of top-class brass teaching in schools throughout the country is making banding popular in areas which have no tradition of brass bands. If this trend continues, as it shows every sign of doing, the grip of the northern bands on the traditional contests may be broken as new regions begin to build up their strengths. There have also been new developments in advanced banding education. The National Youth Brass Band will be discussed further in the next chapter, which will also give some idea of the attitudes of the young towards the music and the band movement. But higher education for bandsmen is, becoming increasingly available, too. Derek Bourgeois has described earlier how a bandsman used his brass band expertise, both in perform-ance and in written work, towards his music degree at Bristol University. Recently the Graduate Diploma in Band Musicianship at the Salford College of Technology has been raised to degree status, to include compositional, analytical and performance studies, as well as conducting, recording techniques and interpretation studies, among many varied choices. A testing and highly advanced course such as this will produce the top players, conductors and composer-arrangers of the future and will ensure that banding continues to flourish and advance.

One of the greatest changes the educational opportunities have brought to brass bands has been the introduction of women into the bands. During the Second World War some women joined bands to fill spaces left by bandsmen in the services; a few stayed, but not in large numbers. Brass teaching in school is open to everyone regardless of sex, however, and the 1960s and 1970s have seen ever-increasing numbers of female musicians joining bands. As we shall see, the National Youth Brass Band has been an important instrument of change, for many of its students are girls, who are more than capable of holding their own and often outshine their male counterparts. These fine female musi-cians are finding it difficult to take their place in the top bands, however, where male chauvinism and tradition appear to be more deeply entrenched than elsewhere; one notable exception is Desford Colliery Dowty Band, who inlcude some women members in their ranks and have proved to be one of the top contesting bands of the last ten years. Women conductors are rather more scarce, although Barbara Stone has conducted top-section bands at leading contests. As girls start to collect degrees in Band Musicianship from Salford, it is to be hoped that we shall see more and more emerge. Banding is changing its attitude towards women, and maybe the time of the 'brass band widow' is passing. The top bands cannot continue to ignore the claims of the best female musicians: they do so at their peril.

12
Chorus

The National Youth Brass Band

THE NATIONAL YOUTH Brass Band was the brainchild of Dr Denis Wright who, after conducting a youth band concert in Leeds in 1950, decided that something should be organized to encourage young brass musicians. So in January 1951 a first council meeting was held and a governing body set up, consisting of representatives from all the banding areas, a musical adviser (Dr Wright himself) and a secretary/chief administrator, Leonard Davies. To add prestige to the fledgling venture, Sir Malcolm Sargent agreed to become the first president. The inaugural course was held in Bradford at Easter 1952; a team of tutors from the band world had been invited to teach the ninety-six students who had applied. So successful was the course that auditions were afterwards introduced in order to deal with the increased number of applications, and to help even out the standards.

The band was extremely fortunate in having Dr Wright as its guiding force, for few people were as well qualified as he to promote and establish the idea. He had been one of the band world's leading composers and arrangers since he had won, with his overture 'Joan of Arc', the competition sponsored by John Henry Iles in 1925 to write the National test-piece; among his other works were the 1933 Belle Vue test-piece 'Princess Nada' and the 1945 National test-piece 'Overture for an Epic Occasion'. In addition to his composing activities, Dr Wright had been 'the brass band man' at BBC Radio before Harry Mortimer, and it is thanks to his pioneering work that many of Harry's ideas were so successful. His position also helped to lend respectability and authority to banding, as his widow, Maud Wright, explains: 'We were lucky that my husband knew people in the orchestral world, so these people would come, not for

203

the money, but out of interest and enthusiasm. When Sir Adrian Boult conducted here on our tenth anniversary it was like the mark of approval for what we had done.'

Finance, particularly lack of it, has always been a problem for the band; Dr Wright had to finance the early courses out of his own pocket. For a time in the 1970s the band received a grant from the Arts Council, but that was only won with a fight (including questions in the House of Commons). Maud Wright told me: 'The Arts Council mandate is not to help amateur organizations but to help professionals. Their explanation in the case of the National Youth Orchestra was that the subsidy it was given was for the professional tutors. So I said that we also had professional tutors, and eventually they gave us £750 a year, which was fine for us because we operate on a shoestring, and that kept us rolling.'

Unfortunately that grant was lost in the late 1970s when the Arts Council cut its grants to forty amateur bodies, including the NYBB, the National Youth Orchestra and the National Jazz Orchestra, and the NYBB has indeed had to survive on a shoestring ever since. A former student is searching for sponsorship for the band, the Performing Right Society gives a grant, as does the Bandsmen's Memorial and Educational Trust, but it is sad to have to say that there is only limited support from the wider world of banding. Maud Wright points to the problem: 'I was talking to David James[1] the other night about ways of funding. I said that if every band in the country gave us a pound a year each, that would be a great help. A band will put on a concert and expect people to pay to see them, but they will not cross the road and pay money themselves to listen to another band perform. It's this blinkered attitude – when we had our jubilee appeal it was the small bands who gave contributions rather than the major ones. Yet when I go to listen to the top-class bands I see our ex-students in those bands. I think that all the lead chairs in Desford Band are held by former NYBB players, to give you just one example.' As we have stated elsewhere, it really is time that the NYBB had the wholehearted support of the band

1 Conductor of Grimethorpe Colliery Band 1985–7

movement, and particularly of the major bands who benefit the most from the existence of a training organization of such high quality.

Today the band is organized in much the same way as it was at its inception. Roy Newsome explains: 'I'm known as the Music Director. We changed the name when I took over, the post formerly being known as the Music Adviser. I'm only the fourth in the band's history – first there was Dr Denis Wright, the band's founder; he was succeeded by Geoffrey Brand; then Arthur Butterworth took over, until 1984 when I came in. We have two residential courses a year and basically it is my job to select the guest conductor, as well as to take the occasional course myself. I also organize the instrumental tutors, for the trombones, cornets and so on, who are leading players in the band world. We have a pool of tutors that we use so the team is always different, although the same faces keep cropping up.'

Students have to audition for a place in the band and, if successful, generally go on to a waiting-list to await a vacancy in whichever section they have applied for. As Roy Newsome explains, the auditions are very tough: 'They have to play some scales and arpeggios, a solo, an extract from a well-known test-piece, and do some sight-reading. We are also looking at character, to see whether they are the right sort of person to fit into the band.'

The waiting-lists have been becoming shorter recently, possibly because of the increase in the number of county youth bands, and the NYBB is having to mount a recruitment drive for the first time in years. This worries Maud Wright. 'The youngsters who came on our course often used to get grants from their local education authorities to pay for their fees, but when the county youth bands started the local authorities funded them instead. We take the view that the aim of youngsters in county youth bands should be to qualify for the NYBB.' Let us hope that both structures can complement each other rather than one putting the other out of business.

Once a student has been accepted into the band, he or she can remain a member until their nineteenth birthday, when they are forced to leave in order to make way for new talent.

The two courses a year are extremely full and demanding, packing a great deal of music-making into one week. Roy Newsome says: 'The course involves a week in residence rehearsing with the guest conductor and in sectional tutorials with the instumental tutors, preparing a programme for the end-of-course concert. We also organize one or two other activities during the week to relieve the monotony, if there is any monotony! There is usually a sight-reading session, when they get two or three pieces and just run through them. We also have an annual competition to find the junior and senior soloists. I sometimes run a little conducting session for those who are interested. There is also an award for any student doing a project not involved with actual playing – occasionally someone might want to have a dabble at conducting, so I set them a couple of assignments, or maybe someone will come up with a composition or arrangement.'

The standard of performance at the end-of-course concert would amaze any music-lover, and the band is just as capable of playing the most modern repertoire as the traditional works of the 1930s and 1940s – often more so than many senior bands. The students are the top bandsmen of the future and deserve all the support that we can give them. As Roy Newsome points out, 'They are all involved in other bands anyway. Of course, over the years many of the top players, both in brass bands and in professional brass playing, have come through this band. It's surprising now how many students come from areas where there aren't any top bands; lots come from the South, for instance. But all of them will remain involved in some way – one of our basic requirements is that they genuinely are brass banders.'

The rest of this chapter is based on interviews with eleven members of the NYBB who were on the summer course at Harrogate College in August 1987. The contributors were:

Judith Hope (19), Washington – percussion (Newcastle Brown Band)
Jeanette Speller (16), London – cornet (Regent Brass)

Clair Roberts (18), Reading – cornet (Charles Church, Camberley)

Ros Hall (18), Northampton – tenor horn (Guildhall School of Music)

Claudia Tomkins (18), Wantage – flugel horn (Halls of Oxford Band)

Lorraine Firth (18), Barrow-in-Furness – baritone (Vickers Barrow)

Stella Greatorex (17), Sherburn in Elmet – trombone (Rothwell Temperance)

Matthew Payne (12), Bingley – percussion (Jayess Queensbury)

Graham Sibley (18), St Ives – bass (about to join Guildhall School Band)

Paul Bottomley (21), Halifax – bass (looking for a band)

James Kowszun (19), Wantage – cornet (about to join Cambridge Co-op Band)

(James and Paul had both left the NYBB, but were back for the day.)

As can be seen from the above, NYBB members come from all over the country. Judith, Ros, Lorraine, Stella, Matthew and Paul from the North, and Graham from Cornwall, come from areas traditionally involved with banding, areas that you would expect to be producing the top young players. However, Jeanette, Clair, Claudia and James are from the South-East and are representative of a generation of brass banders that is emerging in areas with less of a banding tradition. Not surprisingly, none of the 'South-East four' came from a background that could be called particularly 'brass band', but then neither did all the students from the more traditional areas – Matthew, for example, was the first member of his family ever to have played a musical instrument. Brass banding today is an activity open to all, irrespective of background.

This greater availability of opportunity to participate in banding activities is due in part to local education authorities, who have provided peripatetic brass teachers in response to, and to encourage, the growing demand for brass instrumentalists in schools. Not all the students had learnt to play in school, however; in fact, some had not even had teaching available. Claudia, James and Graham had been taught by the bandmaster in the traditional way, and had come to banding either through a brother or sister or through personal enthusiasm, rather than because of facilities organized at school. The students from the North seem to have had the advantage of educational improvements to a greater extent than their friends from the South, although they were worried that existing possibilities might begin to disappear as cuts in education spending become more widespread.

All the students displayed an interesting mixture of views about the brass band movement, for although they showed enthusiasm for new ideas, their general outlook was fairly traditional. They were all great devotees of contesting, especially of the older test-piece contests, even though some of them had only limited experience of the contest platform. They did not seem to feel that banding particularly needed to change its public image in order to attract wider audiences; rather, they thought that the general public needed to change its attitude to brass bands, and that, desirable as a change of attitude might be, banding could carry on quite happily without wider audiences.

On the other hand, in their opinion some changes within the band world are necessary. All the girls have ambitions to play in a top-section band, usually Black Dyke for choice, but said that they had very little chance of doing so because banding at the highest level is such a male-dominated world. They quite rightly believe that they have proved their worth by being in the NYBB, and expect the top bands to treat them with the same respect as they would a male graduate from the band. However, James and Paul seemed rather sceptical as to whether girls would ever be allowed into the hallowed ranks of Black Dyke or Grimethorpe.

Edward Gregson would appear to be the most popular composer among young brass banders, although anyone writing original pieces for brass band won approval. The students were very proud of their original repertoire, all professing to be fans of the modern works in particular. Even so, their tastes within the modern repertoire were somewhat conservative – of the pieces they were rehearsing for the end-of-course concert, they all liked Elgar Howarth's 'In Memoriam RK' (the conductor Rudolf Kempe), but were less enthusiastic about his more avant-garde work 'Ascendit in coeli'. Most of them seemed to think that the old repertoire was music written during the 1960s and early 1970s, but had enjoyed what they had heard of the brass band classics like Percy Fletcher's 'Labour and Love', which they were working on during the course. Generally their attitudes were extremely open-minded and they seemed inquisitive about all original brass band music, old and new.

The NYBB courses are universally popular, and all the students stressed the importance of the musical aspects over all others. Socially, they all enjoy themselves and it is clear that many lasting friendships are made through the band – some claimed that their friends at home, unable to understand their enthusiasm, think they are mad, and so the courses also provide an opportunity to talk banding with a like-minded group (James had returned to visit for the day because he felt starved of bands and band conversation after a year at university). None of them had any serious complaints to make about the courses.

All were adamant that they wanted to stay in banding, and at as high a level as possible. If anything is going to kill off the cloth-cap image once and for all, it will probably be the involvement of these new musicians, for they simply do not fit the stereotyped image of what brass banders are supposed to be. Paul had just graduated from London University with an engineering degree; James had completed his first year at Cambridge University; Stella was hoping to be offered a place on the degree course in band musicianship at Salford College of Technology. Others had hopes of becoming teachers, while others still had different ambitions; but all would play in a band, whatever they ended up doing. Only Graham had ambitions to enter the professional musical world, which would limit his banding activities. Such a diversity of background and ambition, which is becoming increasingly common among brass banders, may well go a long way towards changing the popular conception of what bands do and what the people in them are like.

Finally, before presenting two of the interviews in full, we should like to thank the contributors for their time and patience. Their enthusiasm is infectious; let us hope it remains as contagious throughout the rest of their banding careers.

The first interview was with Stella Greatorex and Matthew Payne.

PATRIC HOWARTH: *Do you come from a 'brass band' family?*

STELLA GREATOREX: My great-grandfather played in Besses o' th' Barn a long time ago, but that's about it, really, as far as brass bands are concerned.

PATRICK HOWARTH: *So how did you get started?*

STELLA GREATOREX: I played baritone first, when I was eight years old – a primary school teacher encouraged me to start. Then I moved on to the euphonium, and I've only just moved on to trombone for this course.

PATRICK HOWARTH: *Did you get your lessons through school? Was the local education authority a help?*

STELLA GREATOREX: Yes, it was very good. I go to Sherburn High School now, which has a pretty good youth band. The school has its own supply of instruments to encourage people to start, and the teaching there is mostly brass, although there is a bit of woodwind and guitar – no other strings, though.

PATRICK HOWARTH: *Do you hope to carry on studying music after school?*

STELLA GREATOREX: I want to go to music college after my A levels. I'm going to audition for a place on the Salford Band Musicianship degree course. But I don't just want to do a performing course. I want to qualify in as many different aspects of music as possible, because I'd like to teach later on, as well as play in a band – or I'd like to examine; in fact, I'd love to be an examiner.

PATRICK HOWARTH: *What about you, Matthew, what is your background?*

MATTHEW PAYNE: I've tried to trace my family back, and none of them has ever played a musical instrument. I was the first one.

PATRICK HOWARTH: *How did you become interested, then?*

MATTHEW PAYNE: Ever since I was three I always seemed to bang about on things, so when I was five I asked for drum lessons. I started private lessons when I was six and have progressed from there.

PATRICK HOWARTH: *What sort of music attracted you to drumming – band music or pop music?*

MATTHEW PAYNE: Pop music, really.

PATRICK HOWARTH: *So how did you come to join your local brass band?*

MATTHEW PAYNE: I found that I was stuck in my room playing along to tapes, and I wanted to get out and play live, so I auditioned for the Jayess Band.

PATRICK HOWARTH: *Do you prefer playing brass band music to pop music now?*

MATTHEW PAYNE: Yes, I do, really. It's better for reading – more technical, more difficult.

PATRICK HOWARTH: *Did you get any lessons through school?*

MATTHEW PAYNE: I did, but by the time I was old enough to have them I'd learnt everything, so they didn't make much difference. I don't have private lessons either any more, I just go through books of exercises every now and then.

PATRICK HOWARTH: *Do you want to keep you drumming and music going after school, and so on?*

MATTHEW PAYNE: Oh, yes. I'd like to go to music college when I'm older, and maybe become a teacher going round lots of schools giving drum lessons. But I'd still keep involved with bands, and play other sorts of music – anything that means playing the drums, really.

PATRICK HOWARTH: *Do you have ambitions to be in one of the top bands?*

MATTHEW PAYNE: I think I'd just like to be in a local band. I'm not that bothered, although right now I'd like to be in Black Dyke.

PATRICK HOWARTH: *What about you, Stella?*

STELLA GREATOREX: I'd like to play in a top band as well as teaching, but it depends whether women are allowed into the highest levels of the band world. It would be great to be in Black Dyke or Grimethorpe.

MATTHEW PAYNE: Lots of the top seats in our band are taken by girls. I think they should be allowed into the best bands.

PATRICK HOWARTH: *Do either of you ever go to concerts?*

STELLA GREATOREX: Not as often as I'd like to, but it's difficult to find the time.

MATTHEW PAYNE: Not really. Only if we are playing in them.

PATRICK HOWARTH: *Do either of you play in contests with your bands?*

STELLA GREATOREX: We play in entertainment contests, area finals for the National and so on.

PATRICK HOWARTH: *What sections are your bands in?*

STELLA GREATOREX: We're in the second section, but I've only been with the band for a year. I was in Milton Brass before that, and we did win at the National about two or three years ago, but were disqualified because of a problem in the percussion section. Sherburn High School has been to London as well, in the Youth section.

MATTHEW PAYNE: We're in the Championship section now; we were promoted last year. The band has been to the National the last four years, and has moved up through the sections.

PATRICK HOWARTH: *Do you enjoy contesting?*

STELLA GREATOREX: I think contests are better than concerts, more exciting. The atmosphere is different, you have to concentrate a lot more.

MATTHEW PAYNE: It's very nerve-racking, but the atmosphere is great, especially when the results come out.

PATRICK HOWARTH: *Don't you find it boring, rehearsing a test-piece all the time before a contest?*

STELLA GREATOREX: Not really. There are so many different things you can get out of it each time – I'd rather do that than rehearse an old concert programme.

MATTHEW PAYNE: We usually get the piece two or three months before the contest. We'll go through it a few times and then let it drop. Then we get it out again a few weeks before and start practising it every night. It

doesn't get too boring that way; it keeps it
fresh for the actual day.

PATRICK HOWARTH: *Don't you think that entertainment contests are more interesting, particularly from
the audience's point of view?*

STELLA GREATOREX: I suppose it's a change, but I prefer
test-piece competitions. You can't understand that, can you?

PATRICK HOWARTH: *Not at all. What music from the brass
band repertoire do you like?*

STELLA GREATOREX: Modern, very modern.

MATTHEW PAYNE: Yes, I don't like the traditional marches
very much.

STELLA GREATOREX: One of my favourite pieces is 'Year of
the Dragon' by Philip Sparke. But I'm not
against the old stuff – I think 'Labour and
Love', which we are doing on the course,
is brilliant. I suppose I like a variety,
really, but the modern music most. I think
a lot of people outside banding are really
surprised, because they think we still play
marches and so on, but if they heard a
concert of the music that we are doing on
this course, for instance, they would realize how much it's changed.

MATTHEW PAYNE: My favourite pieces are 'Doyenne' by
Goff Richards, which is really modern and
has a good beat to it, and 'Galaxies' by
Carl Davis, which is a bit of everything,
very difficult to play and in a big hall really
knocks the audience backwards. I'm not so
keen on the old stuff, though I like some of
the marches we play.

PATRICK HOWARTH: *Is the NYBB the only chance you get of
playing modern works?*

STELLA GREATOREX: No, we play quite a lot, actually. We play 'Galaxies'. We've got quite a young conductor and he's quite interested in new music.

PATRICK HOWARTH: *What do you think is good about the NYBB courses?*

MATTHEW PAYNE: I've learnt a lot about playing different percussion instruments, things I've not known before.

STELLA GREATOREX: This is my seventh course, but the first where I've played trombone, and I've really enjoyed it. It's interesting being in a different section of the band, getting a different view of the band. It's been more special this time ... The size of the band [usually seventy to eighty musicians] means you have to play together a lot more, and so you have to concentrate even more than usual, because it's a lot harder playing with six trombones than with three.

PATRICK HOWARTH: *What is the social side of the course like?*

STELLA GREATOREX: There's always a comedian ... everyone gets on really well, though. We have to work very hard, so there is not much time off, but nobody seems to mind.

PATRICK HOWARTH: *Is there anything you'd like to change?*

STELLA GREATOREX: Raise the leaving age to twenty-one. The Swiss NYBB has just lowered its leaving age from twenty-five to twenty-one. I know you're going out into the big wide world, to college and everything, but I think it would be good to be able to come back, because there is always more to learn.

MATTHEW PAYNE: I've enjoyed everything since the first day I arrived. I've never been bored and am always worn out at the the end of the day.

PATRICK HOWARTH: *Do you think there are enough people like you getting interested in brass bands to ensure their future prosperity?*

STELLA GREATOREX: It all depends on the schools, and any cuts that might come. We've only got one music teacher at our school now, but we used to have two. It's got to come from the schools; that's where I started. If music isn't pushed at school it will just stop; not just brass bands, but orchestras as well.

PATRICK HOWARTH: *What do your friends think about your being in brass bands?*

STELLA GREATOREX: The only trouble is that you end up not knowing what to talk to them about. They get bored if you start talking about contests, because they don't understand. It's good to mix with both band people and other people, because then you get the experience of two different sorts of lifestyles.

MATTHEW PAYNE: Some of my mates come to concerts and really enjoy it, but others think it's really boring, old-fashioned music. They think you're a bit of a weed.

STELLA GREATOREX: If they came to a concert, sat and listened, rather than talking about something they don't know about, I bet they would change their minds.

The second interview was with Graham Sibley.

PATRICK HOWARTH: *Do you come from a brass band background?*

GRAHAM SIBLEY: No. The only other member of my family in a band was my brother, who played the trombone. My parents encouraged me when they saw the success my brother was having with the local band. I didn't want to join the band at first, but my resistance wore down, so I started to go along with my brother.

PATRICK HOWARTH: *How old were you when you started, and did you have your lessons through school?*

GRAHAM SIBLEY: I was twelve or thirteen, and all my teaching came from the band and the bandmaster; I didn't learn at school at all. The bandmaster taught me everything until I reached this level, since when I haven't really had much teaching.

PATRICK HOWARTH: *What are your ambitions after leaving school and the NYBB?*

GRAHAM SIBLEY: I've just finished my A levels and have been offered a place at the Guildhall School of Music in London, so I'll be off there in September.

PATRICK HOWARTH: *Do you hope to become a professional?*

GRAHAM SIBLEY: Yes, with a London orchestra if possible, but the number of professional tuba jobs is very limited.

PATRICK HOWARTH: *If you are successful in turning professional, will you still keep involved with brass bands?*

GRAHAM SIBLEY: Oh, yes. Bands have always been the mainstream for me; in fact, I've not done very much orchestral playing. I would certainly want to be involved with bands if there was time, although as a professional I shouldn't be allowed to play in contests.

PATRICK HOWARTH: *Do you think that banding is still a very traditional world?*

GRAHAM SIBLEY: Banding has tended to move away from traditionalism, I think. However, the area that I come from, Cornwall, has remained very traditional, probably because it is cut off from the mainstream and the new ideas. I think Cornwall is more traditional than the North – the new music seems to have been accepted far more readily in the North than I would have imagined.

PATRICK HOWARTH: *Probably the strongest bastion of tradition is contesting. Do you feel that the contests are still of value to brass bands?*

GRAHAM SIBLEY: I've been to a few contests, although not many, and I think they are wonderful. They both raise and maintain standards. The idea of working on a piece in order to make it as perfect as possible doesn't seem to me a waste of time, although I can understand why some people might think that it is.

PATRICK HOWARTH: *What about the entertainment contests?*

GRAHAM SIBLEY: It is quite interesting to listen to a programme of music written in a variety of styles, especially when the music has been written specifically for an entertainment contest. But I prefer the test-pieces myself.

PATRICK HOWARTH: *What is local contesting like? Are rivalries very fierce?*

GRAHAM SIBLEY: It depends on the situation. If a band

has had a rough time over the past year, because players have left or something, that band will want to show that it is still in the running, and then the competitiveness is very fierce. There was one occasion when I played for a band in St Ives, where fourteen players had just left – over half the band – and we had to go to play in a local contest. We worked like stink with a band of eighteen players, and on the day we were the smallest band there. It was really quite special, because we won both sections and showed the others we were still a force to be reckoned with.

PATRICK HOWARTH: *What repertoire do you like?*

GRAHAM SIBLEY: I like the old test-pieces – 'Labour and Love' is good stuff. I've no real preference between the old and the new music. I like 'Life Divine' and 'Resurgam', but I also like some of the more modern pieces. Some of the very new stuff, like the National test-piece this year ['Diversions' by Derek Bourgeois], strikes me as too manufactured – a sort of 'This is a test-piece and will test every player in the band', rather than being a piece of music.

The earlier sort of entertainment music on the whole is, to put it bluntly, tripe. By earlier I mean the late 1960s and early 1970s. There were some appalling arrangements, which are best left alone. Some of the newer arrangements, however, such as Ray Farr's 'Firebird', are far more interesting both to play and for an audience to listen to.

PATRICK HOWARTH: *Do you think these NYBB courses are valuable?*

GRAHAM SIBLEY: Oh. yes. There are certain things you

hear on each course that you will not have heard before – when you listen to other people play, or even just warming up – and so you think to yourself: 'I'll try doing that.' In fact, you can learn as much from the other students as you can in a tutorial. The problem with the tutorials, which is not the fault of the tutors, is that they are geared to playing a piece at a concert, to getting a decent performance at the end of the week by hook or by crook, even if it means dropping players from the end of the section.

PATRICK HOWARTH: *Do you think that the wider world of banding needs reforming in any ways?*

GRAHAM SIBLEY: There seems to be a shortage of really good conductors. That probably sounds very presumptuous, coming from me. Certainly if there were more to go round it would help the southern bands to develop. The South itself seems to think that there are no good bands in the South, and a lot of very good players don't get the recognition they possibly deserve, because they play with southern bands. If these bands had the best musical directors, I think they would soon be able to give the northern bands a real run for their money, which could only be good for banding in general.

Encore

ENCORE PIECES ARE usually light and amusing, bon-bons for an audience presumed happy at the end of a concert. The band world, as we have seen, is essentially serious, even fanatical, passionate in its dedication and commitment, but it is far from dull. Rehearsals, certainly at Grimethorpe, are intense but liable to erupt into hilarity since wits are sharp and tongues quick. The bandsman's humour is special, sometimes innocent – sometimes not.

Eddie Dawes, the principal cornet player of Barton Hall Works Band when I first joined, and myself, aged about 14, were engaged for a march job in Salford by a local band. It was a hot summer's afternoon. We waited at the main crossroads in Salford for our hosts to arrive, which presently they did in ones and twos, uniforms oddly assorted in a variety of ale-stained pink. March cards were dished out and Eddie and I seemed to be alone on the solo cornets line until at the last moment, as we were about to move off, the stout figure of their own principal solo cornet player bustled forward.

"Lo! You two lads wi' me?'

'Yes.'

'Well, you take t'pianos,' (the softer more lyrical passages, usually the prerogative of the principal) 'and I'll look after t'fortes,' (the louder dramatic bits normally played by 'the others').

We demurred, modesty forbidding that we should steal his thunder.

'You mean the other way round?' Eddie suggested.

'No, no, lad. Not in *this* band!'

He was amazing; for two hours marching across the cobble-stones of Salford, on the hottest day the North-West

221

of England can ever have known, with cheeks bulging and eyes popping, he obtained the fiercest sound I have ever heard from that sweetest of instruments, the cornet.

Harry Birtwistle, the composer, known for his sartorial individuality, arrived at Grimethorpe one very cold day in 1973 in what I seem to remember he said was his grandfather's overcoat. It was a splendid but rather worn relic of a once-proud garment.

He heard his 'Grimethorpe Aria', rehearsed, made one or two characteristically terse but not unfriendly criticisms and retired with most of the band to the Miner's Institute for a beer. Some of the players seemed slightly non-plussed by this famous composer in their midst who enjoyed the Tetley's bitter, wrote such extraordinary music and sported the overcoat. One in particular was mystified. Brian Couling, cornet, was himself something of a nonconformist, but even he found Birtwistle difficult to twig. He looked at him in some amazement; took me to one side.

'Is that Birtwistle's best coat?'

'It's the only one I've ever seen him in.'

Pause – in wonder.   'A wouldn't let me dog sleep on it!'

The humour can be more barbed, and the dedication occasionally missing. A conductor new to Grimethorpe found himself with a week's rehearsals scheduled before Christmas with neither concerts nor contests to prepare. Being young and enthusiastic it seemed to him to be the ideal time to bring out of the library some of the extremely difficult repertoire pieces the band has acquired, knock off the dust and finish the year in a blaze of activity.

His suggestions brought stony silence. Perplexed, he surveyed the twenty-six faces before him. 'Well, what do you usually do at this time of year?'

Silence – then a reply from one of the tubas. 'We usually play a game.'

'Oh, what game?'

'Tha put th'head down on t'music stand, close tha eyes and we all run off and hide.'

Elgar Howarth

Index

223